THE HISTORY OF
Country & Western Music

THE HISTORY OF Country & Western Music

TONY BYWORTH

Exeter Books
NEW YORK
A Bison Book

First published in USA 1984 by
Exeter Books
Distributed by Bookthrift
Exeter is a trademark of Simon & Schuster, Inc.
Bookthrift is a registered trademark of Simon & Schuster, Inc.
New York, New York

ISBN 0-671-06986-1

Printed in Hong Kong

Page 1: Hank Williams, Jr., the legend's son who won out with his own interpretation of country music and a record-breaking eight albums at the same time.

Page 2: 'Rambling' Teddy Baird fingers a B-flat chord on the frets of his Harmony guitar.

Below: On stage at the Grand Ole Opry in the Ryman Auditorium around the early 1950s. Lonzo and Oscar are center stage with the guitar and mandolin.

Contents

Beginnings

Country music had always existed in the South, though it wasn't called 'country' back in those early days. It didn't even have a name, it was just a music of the people . . . a music treasured by the rural white folks of the area, passed on from generation to generation as it had been from the first day that the settlers had made this new land their home and, before that, in the families' British and European birthplaces. The music was relocated and the songs subjected to change through the passing of the years and the chain of singers, but still coming to life after a lengthy day's toil as family and neighbors gathered in homesteads to pass time together. It was the nucleus of merriment at barn dances and traveled between Southern townships by means of wandering musicians and medicine shows. It was truly an indigenous music.

The fiddle was its main instrument. A raisin' of the bow, a hoot and a holler, and the dance was on. The more puritanical members of the community viewed the fiddle as 'the device of the devil' as it aroused the spirits, but the words of damnation were soon overshadowed by the excitement. Later, as more musicians gathered, it would be complemented by guitar and banjo, with the Appalachian dulcimer, autoharp and mandolin playing lesser roles.

In the first two decades of the twentieth century the general population of the States knew little about this music of the South but, with advances in communications, the changes were set to begin. Radio and records played natural roles in its development, with radio breaking down the isolation of the rural areas and records, eventually, providing the musician with an opportunity to pursue a career hitherto impossible.

The music first made progressive strides during the early 1920s. Initially radio made its impression by not only revolutionizing rural existance but also by forging popular tastes, particularly in the South, as this area saw the birth of the greatest number of radio stations. At the same time the fledgling record industry, in an effort to increase its market, started recording local performers with the intention of selling the finished product to the local audiences. Like the black, or 'race,' recordings that had already proven successful, the recording executives' plan was to sell the Southern white man's music to the Southern white population.

The Southeastern region of the States was the common trekking ground of the record men seeking out musicians on their field trips; any one who could play an instrument or sing a rural song was given an audience. At first, virtually all the recordings featured amateur talent. Music was a part of the rural lifestyle and few thought of pursuing it as a profession. It was this rural naturalness that gave the recordings their greatest sales potential. These field trips increased as the decade progressed and were in full swing by the beginning of the 1930s when, owing to the Depression and the booming radio medium, the record industry was dealt a damaging blow. By then it was obvious that the music was maintaining steady sales with a loyal audience. More important, the music had gained an identity with a name – hillbilly – and was building itself a roster of known singers.

Above: **Eck Robertson, champion fiddler, with his flag.**

Strangely enough, the first indication that the music did possess popular appeal didn't come from a recording that originated from the South or, even, from a singer who had any connections with a rural lifestyle. The man in question was Wendall Hall who, in the early 1920s, had taken hold of a dance tune, added novelty lyrics, and released it as *It Ain't Gonna Rain No Mo.* It quickly wound up as one of the most popular releases from the Victor company. Around that time another record company, Okeh, began setting up recording studios in a number of Southern locations, including Atlanta, Georgia, and Bristol, Virginia. The search for talent was on.

Although the first genuine country recording has yet to be determined, it is generally regarded that it was made by a champion

Below: The original Carter family from Virginia included Maybelle Addington, guitarist and vocalist; Sara Carter on the autoharp; and A P. They sang together until 1943.

Above: **Jimmie Rodgers, 'The Singing Brakeman,' was the first star of country and western music. His career was cut short by tuberculosis in 1933.**
Above left: **Once an opera singer, Vernon Dalhart switched to hillbilly and achieved record-breaking success.**

old-time fiddle player named Eck Robertson, a native of Amarillo, Texas. The recording came about quite by accident on the record company's part, when Robertson, together with an old-time fiddle compatriot Henry Gilliland (from Virginia), arrived in Victor's New York offices in June 1922 and stated that they would like to make some records. The request was granted and the recordings subsequently released. It is interesting to note that, a year or so later, Robertson performed a couple of those tunes, *Sally Goodin* and *Arkansas Traveller* on Fort Worth radio station WBAP, this being the first known plug by a rural musician for songs available on record. Eck Robertson didn't record again though until 1930, this time under the auspices of the most famed of recording pioneers, Ralph Peer.

It was almost by accident that the word hillbilly crept into the musical vocabulary, although the actual term (according to an article penned by Archie Green in the *Journal Of American Folklore*) had appeared in print around the beginning of the century as a general term relating to all Southern backwoods' inhabitants. It became connected to the music following a recording session at the Okeh studios (New York) in which a group of musicians, led by Al Hopkins, recorded six numbers for Ralph Peer. After it was all over, Peer asked Hopkins to think of a name for the group. 'Call the band anything you want,' the musician replied, 'we are nothing but a bunch of hillbillies from North Carolina and Virginia anyway.' The songs were listed as recorded by The Hillbillies – and the name stuck for the music in general.

Undoubtedly the man responsible for the greatest growth of the music in its embryonic stages, and the discovery of much of its talent, was Ralph S Peer. His initial interest in music stemmed from the days that he helped out at his father's phonograph store in Kansas City, Missouri. In 1920 he was appointed recording director of Okeh Records and, shortly afterward, started recording songs for the 'race' catalogs which included sessions with negro blues singer, Mamie Smith. The results proved so successful with negro audiences that Peer decided to head South to seek out more negro singers. He arrived in Atlanta, Georgia, but quickly discovered that the city had little to offer him in this field. At the suggestion of an astute local record dealer, Polk Brockman (who was well aware of the hillbilly musicians in the area, and had guaranteed to sell enough records to cover the costs) Peer made a couple of recordings with Fiddlin' John Carson, a former circus man, house painter and part-time moonshiner. Going through the musician's considerable repertoire, Peer recorded two of them, *The Old Log Cabin In The Lane* and *The Old Hen Cracked And The Rooster's Going To Crow*.

'It was so bad that we didn't even put a serial number of the record, thinking that once the local dealer got his supply, that would be the end of it,' Peer later reflected (*Collier's* magazine, 30 April 1938). 'We sent him 1,000 records, which he received on a Thursday. That night he called New York on the phone and ordered 5,000 more to be sent by express and 10,000 by freight. When the national sale got up to 500,000 we were so ashamed we had Fiddlin' John come up to New York and do a re-recording of the numbers.' Once there, the musician recorded twelve more songs and was signed to an Okeh contract.

But if the success of that record appeared amazing, it was but a drop in the ocean compared with *The Prisoner's Song*, recorded in 1924 by Vernon Dalhart almost as an afterthought. Dalhart, a one-time opera turned popular singer, whose fortunes were flagging, viewed hillbilly music as a means of rejuvenating his career and persuaded Victor Records to take a chance on his hunch. *The Wreck Of The Old 97*, a train song, was the singer's choice and when asked to find an accompanying tune, he came up with the manuscript for *The Prisoner's Song*, supposedly written by his cousin, Guy Massey. It turned out to be the biggest selling record in Victor's pre-electric recording history, with sales reputedly nearing the six million mark. From there on Dalhart remained with hillbilly music and became one of its highest-paid singers during the period 1925-31. He later recorded the song for another dozen companies, which brought him royalties of more than $1 million, as well as releasing records under a string of pseudonyms. *The Death Of Floyd Collins* was his other big seller, but his great success as a hillbilly singer eventually slipped away and he died in obscurity in 1948. Nevertheless his contribution to the music has been recognized and he was elected into Nashville's Country Music Hall Of Fame in 1981, with his plaque noting that he 'was the first popular singer to demonstrate the wide appeal and economic potential of country music.'

Closely connected with Dalhart during his first few years as a hillbilly artist was guitarist Carson J Robison, a musician who was also very successful as a composer of event songs. These songs told of past and current news stories and were always popular fare with audiences. Yet, ironically, it wasn't until 1948 that he recorded his best remembered song. That was *Life Gets Tee-Jus, Don't It,* released on MGM Records.

Among the other early hillbilly recording artists were Charlie Poole, an entertainer who had gained a reputation in vaudeville and on medicine shows; Bradley Kincaid, known as the 'Original Authentic Folksong Singer' because of his avowed intention to sing only rural songs; the Atlanta-based Skillet Lickers, comprising the musicianship of Gid Tanner, Clayton McMichon and Riley Puckett; Ernest V Stoneman, composer of the classic *Great Titanic* (another event song) and leader of his own family group, still in business today, two generations later; and another family band, Mainer's Mountaineers, headed by fiddler J E Mainer and banjoist Wade Mainer. Also making their mark were Buell Kazee, Clarence Ashley and Moran Lee 'Dock' Boggs, all banjo players; Cliff Carlisle, whose repertoire went 'from Hawaiian to yodeling to hobo songs to strictly hillbilly music'; and Kelly Harrell, another Ralph Peer discovery and unique among his hillbilly compatriots in that he played no instrument at all.

As the popularity of these, and other, hillbilly artists increased – and their music started being heard in wider areas, thanks to radio – so the number of record executives and organized field trips down South increased. Those seeking out rural talent included W S Fuhri, Frank Walker and, later, Art Satherly (arguably Peer's greatest rival as a talent scout, his discoveries including Gene Autry and Roy Acuff) at Okeh and Columbia; Eli Oberstein at Victor; and Dave Kapp at Decca.

But there was no one to equal Ralph Peer in the discovery of hillbilly talent. He not only helped bring the music to the attention of a vast public but also, as a result, helped preserve the culture of the area. It was in 1927, working at the Victor Talking Machine Company, that he was to achieve his greatest triumph, making two discoveries that would both shape the future of the music and consolidate its commercial footing. The artists were the Carter Family and Jimmie Rodgers, and both found their way to Peer through notices in the local papers (a ploy normally adopted by the field scout when seeking out acts to record). What's even more incredible is that both acts made their initial recordings in Bristol, Virginia, within two days of each other – the Carters on 1 and 2 August, and Rodgers on 4 August.

Jimmie Rodgers' career was tragically short yet, within a six-year period, he recorded 111 songs and sold over twenty million records. Born in Meridian, Mississippi on 8 September 1897, music played little importance in his life to start with and he concentrated his energies on life as a railroad man. The contraction of tuberculosis put an end to such a lifestyle and, by the mid-1920s, he had started recounting tales of the railroad in music, eventually earning him the title of 'The Singing Brakeman.' The first two songs recorded at that famed Bristol session – *Sleep Baby Sleep* and *The*

Above: **Fiddlin' John Carson recorded several songs with Ralph Peer in the 1920s.**
Below: **Mainer's Mountaineers was made up of family members** ***(left to right)*** **Wade, Zeke, Boyd and J E , who headed it up.**

Soldier's Sweetheart – secured him a contract with Victor, with Peer being particularly impressed with the singer's yodeling style. Once the songs were released on record, Victor was swamped with orders and, by the year's end, Rodgers had become the company's biggest selling artist.

He has been described as 'America's truly narrative balladeer' while others view him as the singer who fused the areas of pop, folk, country, jazz and blues. Certainly his recordings contain many different elements in addition to country, with the result that a mass audience was enraptured by his music. His songs detailing trains, railroads and the South found a natural acceptance with rural record buyers, yet proved equally fascinating to those unfamiliar with such themes. *Train Whistle Blues, Any Old Time, Dear Old Sunny South By The Sea, Hobo Bill's Last Ride* and *My Carolina Sunshine Girl* ranked among his output, though his most popular songs were a series of twelve blue yodels which included *Mule Skinner Blues, T For Texas* and *Women Make A Fool Out Of Me.* He even wrote a song about the illness that, on 26 May 1933, finally took his life, *T. B. Blues.*

His music was to be lasting and, along with his distinctive styling, provide a considerable influence on numerous country singers who followed in his wake, including Ernest Tubb (who possesses an original Rodgers' guitar given to him by the singer's widow, Carrie Rodgers), Hank Snow and Merle Haggard (who, in 1969, cut the fine tribute album *Same Train, A Different Time*). When the Country Music Hall Of Fame opened up its doorways in 1961, there was no arguing the fact that this legendary figure deserved to be one of its first members.

The Carter Family lived one of rural music's finest traditions – a family group singing together, first in the intimacy of their own homes and then taking their music out to local events like church socials and school parties. The trio, from Maces Spring, Virginia, comprised A P (Alvin Pleasant) Carter (born 15 December 1891) who sang bass; his wife Sara (born 21 July 1899) who switched between lead guitar and autoharp; and Sara's cousin Maybelle Addington (born 10 May 1909) who, besides adding her voice to the other two, gave the trio its distinctive sound with a guitar styling that used bass strings for melody. Their repertoire consisted of old hillbilly ballads learned from their parents, though A P was resourceful in seeking out other traditional material, as well as being a prolific composer in his own right.

For their audition with Ralph Peer the Carter Family sang six familiar Southern songs, including *Bury Me Under The Weeping Willow, Wandering Boy* and *Little Log Cabin By The Sea,* and it was such emotional output that was to ensure the trio's popularity throughout the years with Victor, commencing with their first professional recording session in 1928. All their recordings sold well, although they didn't have one massive-selling record, and among the 250 songs recorded were *Keep On The Sunny Side, Gathering Flowers From The Hillside, My Clinch Mountain Home, Wabash Cannonball, You Are My Flower,* and A P Carter's originals, *I'm Thinking Tonight Of My Blue Eyes, Lonesome Valley* and *Jimmy Brown The Newsboy.* Just as Rodgers was to influence many later country entertainers, so the Carter Family's songs were to become an essential part of America's musical heritage, being performed in bluegrass festivals and folk events as well as being recorded by artists as diverse as Roy Acuff and Emmylou Harris.

The trio disbanded in 1943, with A P Carter going into retirement (he and Sara were divorced in 1936), and Maybelle continuing working right up until her death in 1978. First she formed a new group with her daughters June, Helen and Anita and then, later, worked shows with her son-in-law, Johnny Cash (who married June Carter in 1968) as well as maintaining a spasmodic recording career. Today there's still a Carter Family group (featuring Helen and Anita and assorted relatives) though, for the original members, posterity was further assured with induction into the Country Music Hall Of Fame in 1970.

Far left: Bradley Kincaid, 'The Kentucky Mountain Boy with his Houn' Dog Guitar,' was the star of Chicago's Eighth Street Theater, one of the sources for country music fans further north.
Left: Dr. Humphrey Bate and the Possum Hunters was the first hillbilly band to appear on the Grand Ole Opry, which launched many careers and became the biggest radio show barn dance in the country.
Bottom: Boyle County, Kentucky Sheriff Raymond D. Stigall and his deputies oversee the capture of a still and its 'shine' in 1940 in the Appalachian hill country.
Below: The same men destroyed this moonshine still in nearby McLean Country on 21 September 1940.

Radio and the Grand Ole Opry

Radio was the great communicator. While records provided a further extension of a musician's career, it was radio that initially allowed them to reach an audience outside their own region. As the years passed, the role of radio was to change, with live performances taking a back seat to the playing of records which, eventually, led to the more complex roles of playlists and chart records that is the mode of operation in the highly competitive world of broadcasting today. In the beginning, though, radio was the greatest asset in the development of hillbilly music, its influence being realized when noted in terms of radio growth in general. Two years after its birth in 1920, the sales of radio had grossed $60 million; by 1929 the figure had risen to an amazing $842 million. Radio was, alongside the automobile, the most influential force in the nation.

Radio's advent in the South provided a natural outlet for country music, and the first station to feature it was WSB in Atlanta in 1922, a city that also gave birth to one of the area's first recording studios (a move spurred on by the nucleus of musicians that had gathered for radio performances). Among the first to be heard were Gid Tanner and the Skillet Lickers, also one of the first acts to be recorded by field scout Frank Walker.

The most important development for hillbilly music on radio was the barn dance – a live hoe-down featuring fiddlers and string bands. Fort Worth's WBAP was the first station to present such a format, 4 January 1923, and created the largest audience reaction in the station's brief broadcasting history.

The first barn dance of lasting significance was the National Barn Dance, aired out of Chicago by WLS (World's Largest Store – the station was originally owned by Sears-Roebuck), and it first hit the airwaves on 12 April 1924. The story goes that it was heard originally when the station's janitor, Tommy Dandurand, produced a fiddle and started playing it when there was nobody else available to go on the air. A healthy audience reaction followed and more shows were staged, with a little more advance planning. The show was eventually named the National Barn Dance and finally found a home at the city's Eighth Street Theater when it was realized that many listeners actually wanted to come along and watch the proceedings. Bradley Kincaid, billed as 'The Kentucky Mountain Boy with his Houn' Dog Guitar,' was its first star. Other discoveries included Gene Autry, Lulu Belle and Scotty and Patsy Montana, 'The Yodelling Cowgirl,' who – with the Prairie Ramblers – was among the early exponents of western swing and the first female singer to sell more than one-million copies of a record, with *I Want To Be A Cowboy's Sweetheart*. The National Barn Dance took a more catholic approach in its presentation and included pop songs and comedians alongside the basic ingredients of folk and hillbilly music.

With the show firmly established, it wasn't long before other radio stations followed suit – a trend that continued for several decades. The Grand Ole Opry was to become the biggest of them all, while others included the WWVA Jamboree from Wheeling, West Virginia, launched in 1933 and featuring Grandpa Jones, Doc Williams and Elton Britt among its stars; the Midwestern Hayride

Right: **Uncle Dave Macon, 'The Dixie Dewdrop,' picking his banjo with his son Dorris. He was the Opry's first singer.**
Below (left to right): **Kenny Baker, Bill Monroe, Vic Jordan, Roland White and James Monroe. The Monroe brothers started their careers singing together.**

(which started life as The Boone Country Jamboree on WLW, Cincinnati) and including the Browns Ferry Four, the Delmore Brothers and Riley Puckett among its attractions; The Old Dominion Barn Dance, transmitted by WRVA in Richmond, Virginia; and The Renfro Valley Barn Dance, originating out of the small Kentucky township and founded by a former WLS music director, John Lair.

Among the barn dances that launched the careers of many post World War II stars were the Ozark Jubilee, from Springfield, Missouri, which was hosted by Red Foley for many years; The Big D Jamboree (from KRLD in Dallas, Texas) was the launching pad for such as Billy Walker, Ray Price, Hank Locklin and Sonny James; and Shreveport's Louisiana Hayride, heard on KWKH, was the first home for many famed entertainers, not least of all Hank Williams and Elvis Presley.

The most famous of them all was the Grand Ole Opry. Its first airing came on 28 November, 1925, just a few weeks after the WSM radio station had commenced transmission in Nashville. Owned by the National Life and Accident Insurance Company (the station's call letters, WSM – We Shield Millions – reflected the company's line of business), the station initially boosted 1000 watt transmission power (these days it's up to 100,000 watt clear channel) and was one of the most powerful stations in the South, a factor that quickly attracted musicians to the city.

The Grand Ole Opry was the brainchild of George D Hay, a former newspaper reporter who had earned the nickname 'the Solemn Old Judge' who, before being appointed the director of WSM, had produced the Barn Dance program on WLS in Chicago. The new show first saw life as the WSM Barn Dance and comprised solely Uncle Jimmy Thompson, an 82-year-old Civil War veteran who claimed he knew a 1000 tunes and 'could fiddle the bugs off a sweet tater vine' – accompanied on piano by his niece, Eva

Left: George D. Hay, the man behind the Grand Ole Opry.
Below: The Ryman Auditorium, built by reformed hell-raiser Tom Ryman, was the home of the Grand Ole Opry from 1941 to 1974, when the Opry was relocated in new facilities outside Nashville.

***Above:* Hank Snow, on stage at the Opry.**

Thompson Jones. Following the broadcast WSM was besieged by musicians who also wanted the chance to be heard and, out of these, Hay selected 25, including Mrs Cline, a zither player, the Crook Brothers (Herman and Lewis, who were still a part of the Opry in the early 1980s), the Fruit Jar Drinkers (who became another stalwart Opry act) and Dr Humphrey Bate, a graduate of Nashville's Vanderbilt University and later organizer of the Possum Hunters, the first hillbilly band to appear on the Opry. In 1926 Hay engaged the show's first singer, Uncle Dave Macon, a 56-year-old entertainer with vaudeville experience who played the banjo with a diverse variety of complex frailing and picking styles and was known affectionately as 'The Dixie Dewdrop.'

In 1927 the WSM Barn Dance became the Grand Ole Opry. By then the show had secured a three-hour running time and followed on from an NBC serious music production, The Musical Appreciation Hour. On this particular evening the Barn Dance commenced with negro harmonica-player DeFord Bailey performing *Pan American* and, upon its conclusion, Hay uttered the immortal words: 'For the past hour we have been listening to music taken largely from Grand Opera . . . but from now on we will present "the Grand Ole Opry".' The name stuck, and Bailey's *Pan American* remained its theme tune for the next fifteen years.

Up until 1938 the show's emphasis was on instruments, the major exception to the rule being its long-running star, Uncle Dave Macon. Then Roy Acuff joined, creating such an impact that his name was soon to become synonymous with that of the Opry itself. Born in Maynardsville, Tennessee (15 September 1903), Acuff made a late entry into music having first set his sights on a baseball career; he had almost signed a contract with the New York Giants when he was struck down by a severe bout of sunstroke. During his convalescence he learned to play the fiddle – and by 1932 had become a member of a traveling medicine show. Then he formed his first band, The Crazy Tennesseans (later to become the Smoky Mountain Boys) and gained regular work on a couple of Knoxville radio stations which attracted enthusiastic enough response to lead him on to the Opry.

By 1943 Acuff was country music's top entertainer, earning around $200,000 per year and delighting audiences with stage performances that combined music with such antics as Acuff balancing his fiddle bow on his nose or flipping a yo-yo out into the crowds. His songs tugged at the emotions of his fans, and cut across the areas of family and home, religion and event themes, with his repertoire including classics such as *Wabash Cannonball, Wreck On The Highway, Night Train To Memphis, The Precious Jewel, Unloved And Unclaimed* and *The Great Speckled Bird.* Record sales of over 30 million and his pioneering role in the music saw to his election to the Country Music Hall of Fame in 1962 and, today even with a serious heart attack behind him, he still continues to delight the Opry audiences and cuts an occasional record.

If Roy Acuff set the trend for vocalists on the Opry, Pee Wee King and the Golden West Cowboys completed the transistion and, within this band's lineup, was a guitarist who sometimes doubled as vocalist. His name was Eddy Arnold and, one evening in 1939, he stepped forward to sing *Mommy, Please Stay Home With Me.* The audience response was deafening and clearly indicated that the vocalist in country music had well and truly arrived. Arnold, who billed himself as 'The Singing Plowboy.' shortly afterward left King's band to commence a career that was to be one of the most phenomenal ever, but more about that later . . . .

Two other veteran entertainers, who both still entertain regularly on the show, are Bill Monroe, who joined in 1939, and Hank Snow, a member since 1950. Both are members of the Country Music Hall of Fame, the former gaining election in 1970 and the latter nine years later.

Bill Monroe (born Rosine, Kentucky, 13 September 1911) was truly an innovator for he is credited for bringing to light (though not inventing) America's only original music – bluegrass. The presentation comprised unamplified instruments and lead handled by banjo, mandolin or fiddle and complemented by high-pitched vocals. Monroe started off his career with his brother Charlie – who played guitar to the other's mandolin – and first gained national recognition in 1934 with *Kentucky Waltz.* When they went their separate ways four years later, Bill Monroe established his band the Bluegrass Boys, a skilled bunch of musicians that, over the years, included such as Lester Flatt and Earl Scruggs (themselves to lead a highly successful band for 21 years until 1969, at which time Scruggs – one of the world's foremost banjoists – moved over to country-rock working with his sons Gary and Randy while Flatt remained with bluegrass), Howdy Forrester (later to join Acuff's Smoky Mountain Boys), Don Reno, Red Smiley, Jimmy Martin and Carter Stanley. Among his other original songs are *Blue Moon Of Kentucky*, which helped Presley on the road to stardom, albeit given a somewhat different treatment, *Uncle Pen* and *Scotland.*

Above: **Early recording artist Harry 'Mac' McClintock sang tunes about cowboys and hoboes.**
Below: **Pee Wee King and his Golden West Cowboys included vocalist Eddy Arnold.**

Looking back to the occasion that Monroe joined the Opry, George D Hay reflected, '. . . he gave us a sample of folk music "as she should be sung and played." There is that authentic wail in his high-pitched voice that one hears in the evening in the country when Mother nature sighs and retires for the night.' Such traditions have remained the basis of the show's popularity over the years.

The far-reaching influence of the Grand Ole Opry, both by the artists that appeared as well as WSM's powerful transmissions, are fully realized by the career of Hank Snow (born Nova Scotia, Canada, 9 May 1914), who had heard the broadcasts from hundreds of miles away. He began his career working small clubs billed as 'Hank, The Singing Ranger,' building up a following strong enough to attract a recording deal with RCA Canada. But it wasn't until 1949 that he secured his first US release and, within one year, had put three records at the top of Billboard's newly launched Country & Western Charts – *I'm Movin' On* (established as his theme song), *Golden Rocket* and *Rumba Boogie*. Other big successes for the nasal-toned singer were *Fool Such As I* (1952), *I Don't Hurt Anymore* (1954), *Tangled Mind* (1957) and *I've Been Everywhere* (1962) and, by the mid-1960s, only Eddy Arnold, Webb Pierce and Jim Reeves had gathered more hits than him. Snow remained with RCA Victor for 45 years, the longest tenure of any artist with any label, with recorded output totaling more than 80 albums and more than 2000 songs and guitar instrumentals.

By the 1940s the Grand Ole Opry had established itself as the king of the live radio shows and the natural home for virtually every artist building success. Among the many artists to make appearances during the 1940s and 1950s were Lester Flatt & Earl Scruggs, Ray Price, Don Gibson, Jean Shepard, 'Little' Jimmy Dickens, Hank Locklin, Faron Young, Johnny Cash, the Everly Brothers and Porter Wagoner, while the 1960s welcomed such as Tex Ritter, Skeeter Davis, George Hamilton IV, Dottie West, Bobby Bare, Billy Walker, Sonny James, Tompall & The Glaser

Above: When he's off stage, country and western singer and songwriter Roy Drusky devotes much of his time to dog breeding.
Right: Bill Monroe, the father of bluegrass music, now presents his annual Bean Blossom Festival. He organized a band called the Bluegrass Boys in 1938 that, over the years, has included some of the foremost country and western musicians.
Below: The masterful entertainer Marty Robbins made his mark as the singer of many different kinds of country music and as a stage performer who aroused his audiences to standing ovations.

Brothers, Jim & Jesse, Jim Ed Brown, Jack Greene, Jeannie Seely and Dolly Parton.

As the cast list grew more and more spectacular, so the listeners' desire to see the show in action grew stronger, with the Opry continuing to seek out ever larger auditoriums in order to seat the crowds. It happened right from the start when the program was broadcast from the fifth-floor studio of the National Life and Accident Insurance Company. As the crowds began to jam the building's corridors, a specially designed studio (Studio C) was constructed to hold 500 people; it soon became too small and the the Opry moved to the Hillsboro Theater, a disused movie house, and from there to a rundown tabernacle in East Nashville. In 1939 the newly constructed War Memorial Auditorium was hired but once again it could hardly seat the crowds and, four years later, the Ryman Auditorium (a 3000-seat auditorium built in 1892 by Tom Ryman, a reformed hell-raising riverboat captain) became its home for over 30 years. Today the Ryman is one of Nashville's popular tourist attractions.

In 1974 the Grand Ole Opry was relocated as the centerpiece of the 400-acre Opryland complex, situated some eight miles outside Nashville. The lavish 4400-seat Opry House is adjoined by a theme park, television studios and one of the South's most massive, luxurious hotels. The name, naturally enough, is the Opryland Hotel.

The Grand Ole Opry, to the first-time visitor, appears an uncontrolled, disorderly affair in which singers, musicians and invited guests mingle in the wings and around the back of the stage as the star attraction is out front singing one of his, or her, famed hit songs. A radio announcer is seen on the stage left, and the show is split into 15- and 30-minute sections, each hosted by an Opry star (who introduces various guests) and sponsored by commercial advertisers. Because of this informality, frequently heightened by the artists giving dedications to members of the audience, the Opry operates almost like a casual gathering of friends, with the show's stars as the beloved heads of a loyal family that's grown substantially over the years.

A warm and enthusiastic audience response is guaranteed, which increases the more the artist is seen and the songs heard. Such was the case of long-time favorite Marty Robbins (born Glendale, Arizona, 25 September 1926), who joined the show in 1953. Frequently, if he were on last, he'd continue his show-stopping performances into the early hours, long after the official midnight closedown time. Singing, songwriting, musicianship, acting and industry business were among his many talents, with car racing a compelling interest that he continued up to his death in December 1982, in spite of having had open-heart surgery several years earlier.

Robbins began his musical career after discharge from the Navy (where he learned to play guitar and write songs), and made the first steps up the ladder by earning himself his own television show, Western Caravan, in Phoenix during the late 1940s. A record deal with Columbia came shortly afterward and, in 1953, he made his chart debut with *I'll Go On Alone.* Three years later came *Singing The Blues* which also put the Robbins name before pop-record buyers, and he kept it that way with *A White Sports Coat (And A Pink Carnation)* and *The Story Of My Life* (both 1957) though it was in 1959 that he really broke into the bigtime with the million-selling *El Paso*, a story song that was to trigger off other original western tales and two best-selling 'Gunfighter Ballads' albums. The singer's skills knew few boundaries and he successfully recorded pop standards, rockabilly, Hawaiian music and ballads in addition to normal country fare. *Don't Worry* (1961), *Devil Woman* (1962), *Ruby Ann* (1962), *Ribbon Of Darkness* (1965) and the powerful ballad, dedicated to his wife Marizona, *My Woman, My Woman,*

Left: 'The King of Country Music,' Roy Acuff sings one of the traditional-style songs that earned him his reputation.
Above and below: Minnie Pearl trades jokes with Roy Acuff on the stage at the Grand Ole Opry. Her routines are famous because of her distinct style of humor.

My Wife (1970) were among his initial Number 1s, while *El Paso City* and *Among My Souvenirs* put him back on top in 1976. He gained election to the Country Music Hall of Fame in 1982, just a couple of months before his death; just rewards for a legend who viewed his role in country music as 'better than working for a living.'

Another long-time, popular attraction is Porter Wagoner (born West Plains, Missouri, 12 August 1930) who, at one time, was instantly recognizable by his colorful rhinestone costumes featuring cacti and wagon wheels within its design. He's also well known for bringing Dolly Parton to national attention and, with her, scored over 20 chart duets including the Number 1 *Please Don't Stop Loving Me* (1974). His own chart status on RCA is considerable, kicking off with *Satisfied Mind* in 1955 and following up with such as *Eat, Drink And Be Merry* (1955), *Misery Loves Company* (1962), *Skid Row Joe* (1965) and *The Carroll County Accident* (1968). Nicknamed 'The Thin Man From The Plains,' he first gained attention via another radio show, Ozark Jubilee. In 1960 he commenced his long-running syndicated television show, which also featured the talents of his road band, The Wagonmasters, and (before Dolly Parton) featured singer Norma Jean.

While the original intention of the Grand Ole Opry was to sign musicians for its barn-dance format, the emphasis later went over to vocalists and, after the war, many artists were signed on the strength of regional successes – or, even, hit records. Texan Billy Walker already had a hit record under his belt – *Thank You For Calling* (1954) – and exposure on many other radio shows. He joined in 1960 and his biggest successes, including the top-rating *Charlie's Shoes* (1962) and *Cross The Brazos At Waco* (1964), were to follow. Jack Greene had had plenty of Opry experience working as Ernest Tubb's drummer in the Texas Troubadours before he joined the Opry and developed as one of country music's biggest stars in the 1960s. He achieved Number 1s with *There Goes My Everything* (1966), *All The Time* (1967) and *Statue Of A Fool* (1969), among others, as well as collecting a stack of trade and public awards. On the other hand, Roy Drusky and Stonewall Jackson came to the show prior to any sort of record success. Drusky, whose smooth voice perfectly suits ballads but who occasionally belted out an uptempo novelty like *Peel Me A Nanner* (1963), found success as a songwriter first, his break coming when Faron Young cut his *Alone With You* (1958). This opened the doors to the Opry and a record contract that quickly achieved a country and pop hit with *Three Hearts In A Triangle* (1961). Jackson also arrived on the show through songwriting skills; his place was secured on the recommendation of music publisher Wesley Rose in 1956. Three years later he had a million-selling hit with *Waterloo*, opening up a career that saw more than 36 chart appearances in the following ten years.

The show also reflects the varied sounds of country music, with bluegrass finely represented by such as Jim & Jesse (McReynolds), The Osborne Brothers and Jimmy Martin in addition to its father figure, Bill Monroe. Jim & Jesse, together with the Virginia Boys, have frequently adopted a more liberal, free-wheeling style of presentation and achieved a number of chart records including *Cotton Mill Man* (1964), *Diesel On My Tail* (1967) and *Freight Train* (1971). Another variation of country is cajun, a hybrid music that originated from the French settlers in Nova Scotia who later relocated themselves in Louisiana. The fiddle and accordian originally dominated the presentation but its current champion, Jimmy C Newman, has combined it with country in his performances with his band Cajun Country. A genuine cajun, Newman secured his first success as a country singer with songs like *Cry Cry Darling* (1954) and *A Fallen Star* (1957, which also made the pop charts), though later offerings such as *Alligator Man* (1961) and *Boo Dan* (1969) brought him back to his roots. He's also built up a substantial following in Europe, especially in Britain where he's made several appearances.

Above: **The Grand Ole Opry as it is today.**
Left: **Another of the Opry stalwarts, Porter Wagoner is as well known for his colorful stage outfits as for his long-running television series, not forgetting his role in bringing to attention Dolly Parton.**

There's also variety to be found in the type of artists appearing on the Opry; humor is provided from such as Minnie Pearl, famed for her high-pitched 'howdy' and patter about 'ketching a feller;' the homespun philosophy of Archie Campbell; breezy instrumental sessions from pianist Del Wood, still winning wild applause for her 1951 hit *Down Yonder*, and guitarist Billy Grammar who went near to the top of the charts with *Gotta Travel On* eight years later. The Ralph Sloan Dancers and the Stoney Mountain Cloggers bring some nifty footwork to the proceedings, and basic country traditions remain the essential ingredient of Grandpa Jones' performances, a banjoist who once worked with Bradley Kincaid in the 1930s.

Although the Grand Ole Opry plays a far less important role in the contemporary country-music scene, it still attracts a number of today's top stars who revere the music's heritage and want to be a part of the most famous country music show of 'em all. Recent additions to the cast list have included Larry Gatlin, Barbara Mandrell, Ronnie Milsap, Ricky Skaggs and Don Williams. A couple of other new members, Boxcar Willie and Riders In The Sky, are much more closely linked to the roots – Boxcar recalling the songs of Jimmie Rodgers and Hank Williams alongside his own original songs, and the Riders (Doug Green, Fred LaBour and Woody Paul) lovingly conjuring the atmosphere, and humor, of the west.

Just as important is the loyalty of the audience. It's hard to estimate the numbers who still tune in to the Grand Ole Opry on Saturday nights, but figures reveal that 900,000 travel to Nashville each year to see the Opry stars in action on stage, and it has been estimated that an additional seven to eight million see Opry stars as they travel around the States. Perhaps the show doesn't hold the prominence of bygone days, but one can hardly overlook such loyalties. To these fans the Grand Ole Opry is still what *real* country music is all about!

Western Swing and the Singing Cowboys

The 1930s added the western to country music and a new term in the encyclopedias – country and western. The decade saw the growth of western swing and the birth of the singing cowboys in Hollywood. Both had a tremendous impact, though they had different origins, western swing being a music peculiar to the southwestern states and the singing cowboy a brain child of the movie moguls.

The growth of the western image occurred mainly in Louisiana, Oklahoma and Texas. The cowboy was one of the most romantic figures of the twentieth century; the last hero to represent total freedom as he roamed the wide-open spaces. He presented an image that was to remain with country music for several decades and one that has seen a comeback during recent years as artists like Waylon Jennings, Ed Bruce and Don Williams, with stetsons worn proudly, all help to keep the image alive and healthy.

Western swing was a music of the cowboy, a good few steps removed from the hillbilly music of the southeastern states, and owed as much to blues and jazz as it did to country. Texas was the most important breeding ground, a not too surprising fact as it was a melting pot of different cultures that included Negro, German, Mexican and Louisiana Cajun. The Lone Star State was also the birthplace of many of country's leading performers, both past and present.

Bob Wills (born Limestone County, Texas, 6 March 1905) was the acknowledged father of western swing and a star figure. On stage, dressed in a white suit, expensive boots and a stetson, with a large cigar in his mouth, he led his band with catchphrases like 'Ah hah, San Antone' (after his 1940 million-selling *San Antonio Rose*, later to become a two-million selling hit for Bing Crosby). He presented a music that cut across boundaries and included blues, jazz and country hoe-downs as well as sacred and pop songs. The name Wills was enough to cram dancehalls and ballrooms with frenzied fans, many of whom might have traveled more than one-hundred miles to see the man and his band in action.

He was a fiddle player whose early life provided as much variety as the music he was later to perform, with occupations that included cotton picking, rough riding, preaching, performing at medicine shows and, even, hanging out with a gang of outlaws. In 1932, along with fiddle player Herman Arnspiger and vocalist Milton Brown, he formed the Light Crust Doughboys under a sponsorship deal with Birrus Mills, a flour company, which led to Fort Worth radio spots on WBAP and a record deal with Victor. But, with popularity secured, Wills left the band within a couple of years and headed out to Tulsa, Oklahoma, where he formed his own group, The Texas Playboys, and started to build his music imaginatively, using a basic lineup of guitars, fiddle and banjo, added to it with piano, drums and a brass section and other instruments where appropriate. Among the musicians who played with him during the formative years were Leon McAuliffe (who popularized the steel guitar in country music, and earned for himself another Wills' catchphrase, 'take it away, Leon'), Jesse Ashlock (fiddle), Al Strickland (piano) and Eldon Shamblin (lead guitar), while vocalist Tommy Duncan, 'the Dean of Western Swing,' gained himself the reputation of being the first crooner in country music. Over the years, and a career that took him across the States to the West Coast and back, Wills and the Texas Playboys recorded for a variety of labels, including Okeh, Columbia, MGM, Decca and Liberty, as well as making numerous transcription recordings. He literally cut hundreds of titles, with *San Antonio Rose, Time Changes Everything, Take Me Back To Tulsa, Texas Playboy Rag, Worried Mind* and *Lone Star Rag* being just some that spring instantly to mind.

Initially Wills' biggest rival was fellow Doughboys compatriot Milton Brown, who had formed his own band, The Musical Brownies, which continued to remain in business for several years after their leader's tragic death in an auto accident in 1936. Their music was more directly linked with jazz, a presentation that was also favored by other western-swing bands like Leon Selph & the Blue Ridge Boys, Ted Daffan and his Cowboys and the Bar-X Cowboys. The Light Crust Doughboys also remained active and gained national attention as their boss man, W Lee 'Pappy' O'Daniel, an executive of Birrus Mills, used them in a political campaign that took him first to the Governorship of Texas and, later, to the US Senate.

Right: **'It doesn't matter who's in Austin cuz Bob Wills is still the king,' attests Waylon Jennings, a giant of today's country music scene. Bob Wills was acknowledged as the father of western swing music, which originated in his state of Texas, but he was a versatile singer whose music was not confined to one type.**

Other bands pushing the western-swing sound included Bill Boyd and the Cowboy Ramblers, Adolph Hofner and his Texans, Jimmie Revard and the Oklahoma Playboys, the Tune Wranglers and the Hi-Flyers. Bob Wills' brother, Johnny Lee, after working with the Texas Playboys for a while, quit the group to form his own western orchestra, as did Leon McAuliffe, who later created the Cimarron Boys.

Meanwhile Texas, an innovative force in the creation of western swing, was developing a new brand of country in the saloons and taverns spread around the area – honky tonk. A new breed of singer was needed to sing a new king of song within these haunts, where heavy drinking and fighting fitted alongside loud conversation and dancing. After all, traditional hillbilly themes about home and the country church were hardly appropriate in such surroundings, nor would they much appeal to hell-raising oil workers out for a good time. Such venues also encouraged changes in the music itself, with the singer and the band – out of a necessity to make themselves heard – making their sounds louder by means of electrified instruments and a more solid rhythm. It was a hard knocks' school for the novice singer, but created a style that, within a few years, would become the dominant force in country.

Ernest Tubb (born Crisp, Texas, 9 February 1914) perfectly exemplified honky-tonk music and was the first to achieve national prominence as well as being one of its most influential stylists. He made his radio debut in 1932 on San Antonio station KONO. There he became friendly with Jimmie Rodgers' widow, Carrie, who provided him with encouragement and the opening to a Victor contract. His first recordings were suitable tributes – *The Passing Of Jimmie Rodgers* and *Jimmie Rodgers' Last Thoughts* (1936), released on the Bluebird label. The start of his long and successful association with Decca commenced in 1940 when he recorded

Blue Eyed Elaine and, shortly afterward, came his million-selling theme song, *Walking The Floor Over You*, which opened up the doors to national stardom, Hollywood and the Grand Ole Opry.

The possessor of a highly distinctive, gravelly voice, Tubb found a regular place in the newly launched charts with records like *Slippin' Around* (1949), *Blue Christmas* (1949), *Missing In Action* (1952), *Thanks A Lot* (1963) and *It's Been So Long Darling* while the many artists he's recorded with have included the Andrew Sisters, Red Foley and, in the 1960s, Loretta Lynn. Always a popular touring attraction – at one time traveling more than 100,000 miles a year – he's also made his mark as owner of the world-renowned Ernest Tubb Record Shops in Nashville and presenter of the weekly Midnight Jamboree radio show which takes to the air after the closedown of the Grand Ole Opry. In 1965 he was made a member of the Country Music Hall of Fame.

As the 1930s progressed many of the western-swing and honky-tonk artists moved westward, establishing a new home on the West Coast. The reason for the decision to move was obvious; they were following their audiences. California had become a prime location for vast numbers of migrant workers from the Southwest, people who had moved on because of the Depression and environmental conditions, especially those from the Dustbowl region of Oklahoma, taking with them their meager chattels and a great love of their native music.

By 1943 Bob Wills, after being discharged from the Army on account of poor physical condition (no doubt assisted by hectic work schedules), had purchased a ranch in San Fernando Valley and was breaking box-office records all over again. But he wasn't having it entirely his own way and had to compete with the bands of such as Spade Cooley and Hank Penny. But there was room for all, and the western-swing outfits were attracting crowds of 10,000 or

Above: **The Light Crust Doughboys in the 1930s. Bob Wills, second from right, left after several years to form The Texas Playboys.**
Above left: **Milton Brown, at the microphone, and Bob Wills, second from left. In 1932 the two formed the Light Crust Doughboys.**
Below left: **Carl T Sprague sang genuine cowboy music in the 1920s and became known as America's first singing cowboy.**
Below: **Hawkshaw Hawkins had a brief but fast-paced career.**

Above: **Jimmy Wakely, far right, had his own band but turned to a career in the movies as 'The Melody Kid.'**
Right: **Spade Cooley was a member of Jimmy Wakely's band in the early 1940s and later established his own group. He began his music career as a classical cellist.**

more at locations like the Venice Pier in Santa Monica and Redondo Beach.

Spade Cooley (born Grand, Oklahoma, 22 February 1910) was Wills' biggest rival, although his music was slicker and a little nearer to the pop sounds of the day as he substituted a three-fiddle lineup in place of horns, frequently giving them special arrangements in lead parts. He also brought in the harp and accordion and offered a selection of material ranging from waltzes to jitterbugs, thus providing instant appeal to ballroom audiences. He made the bigtime when he and his orchestra held down an unprecedented 74-week run, attracting 8000 weekly, at Santa Monica's former white elephant, The Venice Pier.

Cooley's story was, indeed, a tragic one. A classically trained cellist converted to the violin through his love for country music, he briefly worked with Roy Rogers before joining the Jimmy Wakely western band in 1942. When Wakely moved on to a movie career with Universal Pictures, Cooley formed his own outfit employing Tex Williams as its main vocalist (in 1946 Williams signed a recording deal with the fledgling Capitol label and quickly secured a million seller with *Smoke, Smoke, Smoke*). Cooley first recorded for Columbia and, on his initial session, cut *Shame On You*, his biggest hit, which led to the orchestra being increased to 17 members and the establishment of his own Saturday-night television show on KTLA, reputedly one of the most popular shows ever in Los Angeles. In the late 1950s he began developing a recreational park that was to be known as 'Spade Cooley's Water Wonderland' but, within two years, was sentenced to life imprisonment for the murder of his second wife, Ella Mae. On 5 November 1969, with the news of a parole coming up, he was granted leave from Vacaville Prison to perform at a sheriff's benefit in Oakland, California. He once again picked up his fiddle to play in public but, during the intermission, died of a heart attack.

Hollywood, being quick to capitalize on anybody with a sellable name, also started making use of many country stars' talents in the 1940s, frequently featuring artists in supporting roles in low-budget movies. Ernest Tubb was seen in a couple of 1942 western productions, *Fighting Buckaroo* and *Ridin' West*, with Charles Starrett and, a few years later, found more obvious vehicles in *Jamboree* and *Hollywood Barn Dance*. Roy Acuff kicked off an eight-picture, two-week shooting schedule deal with *Grand Ole Opry* (actually filmed in Nashville) in 1940, while Bob Wills began his Hollywood career that same year with *Take Me Back To Tulsa*, which featured his Texas Playboys as well as Tex Ritter in the lead role. He followed up with *Go West Young Lady* (1941), starring Glenn Ford and Penny Singleton, before signing an eight-picture deal with Columbia for a series of westerns, with music provided by Texas songwriter Cindy Walker (later to write country standards such as *In The Misty Moonlight* and *Distant Drums*, as well as contributing to the Wills hit *Bubbles In My Beer*).

The movie capital was also quick to develop its own genre, the singing cowboys, building up its own star roster although the music

Best wishes t
my good Frien
J. L. Franks.
thanks for a
the Help y
Been to
Western
Sincerel
Spade

Above: **Roy Rogers, one of the well-known singing cowboys, followed in the footsteps of Gene Autry.**
Below: **Sons of the Pioneers, formed in 1934, originally included Roy Rogers.**
Right: **Gene Autry was a well-established singer before he became a Hollywood star.**

owed more to pop than to country music, with the songs being written by writers contracted to the studios. But these weren't the first singing cowboys. The originals were directly related to the Old West and offered a different kind of music than that heard from the hillbilly singers of the southeast. In fact some of the first collections of printed songs comprise cowboy material – Nathan Howard Thorpe's 'Songs Of The Cowboy' (1908) and John A Lomax's 'Cowboy Songs And Other Frontier Ballads' (1910) – with Carl T Sprague, Goebel Reeves and Jules Verne Allen being among the first Texans to sing the authentic music of the cowboys. Sprague is generally regarded as being 'America's first singing cowboy' and recorded *When The Work's All Done This Fall* in 1925 for Victor after hearing Dalhart's *The Prisoner's Song* in the belief that he could do as well with a cowboy song. He wasn't far wrong; the record just missed a million sales before the year was out.

Harry McClintock was another of the early recording artists, his material covering themes of the cowboy and the hobo though his best-known songs – *Hallelujah, I'm A Bum* and *Big Rock Candy Mountain* – were somewhat removed from the genre. Otto Gray and his Oklahoma Cowboys were among the first of the western-swing bands and presented such songs as *She'll Be Coming Round The Mountain* and *The Cowboy's Lament.* Zeke Clements, a one-time member of the Cowboys, spoke of Gray as being 'twenty years ahead of his time' and noted the group as being 'both riding, roping, shooting, bronco busting cowboys and musicians as well.'

Undoubtedly the most well-known act was the Sons Of The Pioneers, a fine harmony group formed in 1934 by Bob Nolan, Tim Spencer and Roy Rogers, though Rogers' association was to be relatively shortlived as movies soon beckoned him. The group continued to gain popularity under Nolan's direction, expanded to six members and landed a long-term contract with Victor. Among their most popular songs were *Cool Water, Tumbling Tumbleweeds* (both penned by Nolan and destined to earn him considerable royalties from the various versions recorded over the years), *Home On The Range, Lie Low Little Doggies* and *At The Rainbow's End.* Other members of the Pioneers included Lloyd

To
Laura Lee
Always Best
Wishes
Gene Autry

Perriman, Hugh and Karl Farr, Pat Brady (later to achieve fame in many of Roy Rogers' movies) and Ken Curtis, best known as 'Festus' in the 'Gunsmoke' television series.

Meanwhile Hollywood was establishing the singing cowboy as a popular box-office attraction. The movement started with actors who sang an occasional song in their movies rather than singers who talked dialogue between the songs. Surprisingly, John Wayne is credited as being 'the first singing cowboy' (with his voice dubbed); he created the character of 'Singin' Sandy' in a forgettable Republic offering. But it was Ken Maynard who brought music into the westerns, handling it in an unobtrusive manner that never interfered with the plot. He also recorded for the Columbia Gramaphone Company, but it was soon to go bankrupt and only one record – *Cowboy's Lament* with *Lone Star Trail* – was ever released.

It was Gene Autry (born Tioga, Texas, 29 September 1907) who set the genre in action, though he wasn't a product of the Hollywood star system and did in fact possess solid country qualifications before gaining a bit singing role in a 1934 Maynard movie, *In Old Santa Fe*, which launched him into stardom and set the trend for more than 100 pictures for Republic and Columbia during an eighteen-year period. He credits humorist and philosopher Will Rogers as being the person who encouraged him to seek out a singing career (they met during the days that Autry worked as a railroad telegraph operator). Autry gained initial recognition through appearances on the WLS Barn Dance as 'Oklahoma's Singing Cowboy.' This led to a recording deal with Art Satherley of ARC (American Recording Company) and the release of *That Silver Haired Daddy Of Mine* (1931), a duet with co-author Jimmy Long that sold over half-a-million copies during its first few months on release, and more than five million overall. Other big hits followed, including *Yellow Rose Of Texas* (1933), *Mexicali Rose* (1936), *Back In The Saddle Again* (1939) and *South Of The Border* (1940), though his biggest hit of all had no western connections. The title was *Rudolph The Red Nosed Reindeer* and sales over the years have totaled around ten million.

Then the movies caught up with him. Herbert J Yates, head of Mascot Studios (later to become Republic), and producer Nat Levine were responsible for the introduction of the singing cowboy, a concept that was to furnish 'wholesome' entertainment in the wake of the Hays office clamping down on the sex and scandal that prevailed in Hollywood, both on and off the screen. Of the many hopefuls auditioned, Autry was chosen because of the success already achieved on radio and record, and he gained his first starring role in a science-fiction/western serial titled *Phantom Mountain* (1935) in which he portrayed a singing cowboy named Gene Autry! Among the many pictures he made for Republic were *Tumbling Tumbleweeds* (1935), *Oh Susanna* (1936), *Rootin' Tootin' Rhythm* (1937) and *Melody Ranch* (1940) and, from 1947, proceeded to make movies for Columbia under his own banner, Gene Autry Productions. The association commenced with *The Last Roundup*, which the singer cites as his own particular favorite.

From 1937-42 he was the top money-making western star, with his horse Champion almost as famous as its owner, and – as a singing cowboy – became a millionaire several times over. He engaged in many other business enterprises in the 1950s and 1960s, including the founding of television, recording and music publishing companies, the purchase of a chain of radio stations and

Above left: **In 1937 Gene Autry, one of America's top western stars in the 1930s and 1940s, was photographed alongside Art Satherley of the American Recording Company.**
Left: **Floyd Tillman became famous as a country-music songwriter.**

part ownership of the Los Angeles Angels baseball team. He was elected President of Nashville's Country Music Association in 1963 and, six years later, gained membership into the Country Music Hall of Fame.

The man who took over from Autry as top western star (when Autry was serving in the Army Air Corps) was the 'King Of The Cowboys,' Roy Rogers (born Cincinnati, Ohio, 5 November 1912). He began his musical career by singing and playing guitar at local square dances before becoming a founding member of the Sons Of The Pioneers. Initially he got turned down at a Republic Pictures audition, but got a second chance when he sneaked in with a crowd of extras and landed his first starring role in *Under Western Stars* (1938) as replacement for Autry, who was striking for more money. Subsequently he made 88 more low-budget movies for Republic and broke into the financial bigtime in 1952 by supporting Bob Hope and Jane Russell in Paramount's *Son Of Paleface.* His wife, Dale Evans, starred in many of the movies, commencing with *The Cowboy And The Senorita* (1944), and his horse Trigger was always assured star billing.

Although a fine singer and yodeler, Rogers never achieved any real success with the recordings he made for Victor in the 1930s and 1940s, and is possibly best known for the novelty *A Four Legged Friend.* In 1975 he made a brief comeback with a Top 15 country hit, *Hoppy Gene And Me* (from the reflective album *Happy Trails To You*) and a straight acting role in *MackIntosh And T.J.* which featured soundtrack music by Waylon Jennings. Otherwise most of Rogers records in recent years have been religious duets with his wife.

The third of the legendary singing cowboys was Tex Ritter (born Panola County, Texas, 11 January 1907) whose musical career commenced while studying law at the University of Texas. There he created a lecture and song program, 'The Texas Cowboy and his Songs,' which led on to touring and radio spots and, in the early 1930s, a lead role in the New York production of *Green Grow The Lilacs* (later to emerge as the musical *Oklahoma*). With a reputation established, the next stop was Hollywood, and *Song Of The Gringo* (1936) commenced a two-year, twelve-picture deal with the newly formed Grand National Pictures. He subsequently made movies for Monogram, Columbia, Universal and PRC (Producers Releasing Corp), notching up a staggering total of 58 productions in nine years (more than any other singing cowboy), though none of them were particularly memorable. In 1941 he married Dorothy Fay, his leading lady in two of his movies, *Sundown On The Prairie* and *Rollin' Westward.*

But while Ritter never made it into Autry and Rogers' league, he did succeed as a top-selling country recording artist, being one of the first artists to sign with the newly launched Capitol label and achieving quick success with songs such as *There's A New Moon Over My Shoulder, Boll Weevel* and *Deck Of Cards.* However, it was the recording of the Academy Award-winning theme from the 1952 Gary Cooper movie *High Noon* that put him on the international map as a singer. Subsequently he made frequent television appearances, including his own Tex Ritter's Ranch Party (1957/58), received high chart placings with songs such as *I Dreamed Of A Hillbilly Heaven* (1961) and *Just Beyond The Moon* (1967) and made several albums devoted to western songs. He was made a member of the Country Music Hall of Fame in 1964 and the following year, joined the Grand Ole Opry. Tex Ritter died on 2 January 1974, but the acting traditions are carried on by his

Above right: **Rex Allen was one of the last of the singing cowboys, whose golden age had peaked by the 1950s.**
Right: **In the 1980s his son Rex Allen Jr. made a name for himself among country and western singers.**

Above: Three great names in country music come together. Roy Acuff (left), godfather of country music and proprietor of the Grand Ole Opry, stands beside Ernest Tubb and Tex Ritter. In 1983 Ernest Tubb, Waylon Jennings and Hank Williams Jr. cut a record together.

son John who gained stardom in the high-rating Three's Company television series.

Among the other successful singing cowboys were Jimmy Wakely and Johnny Bond, both of whom also secured success as recording artists. Wakely appeared in more than 70 movies, and many as a character named 'The Melody Kid.' He had a number of hits as duet partner to Margaret Whiting, including the Number 1 rated *Slippin' Around* (1949), while Bond was frequently seen as Autry's guitar-playing sidekick as well as appearing on the star's Melody Ranch program for fourteen years. A prolific songwriter, Bond penned over 400 songs, including the standard *Cimarron* and achieved a chart-topping single in 1965 with the humorous narration *Ten Green Bottles.*

The last of the singing cowboys was Rex Allen, 'The Arizona Cowboy,' a one-time member of Chicago's National Barn Dance. He began his 32-movies career with Republic with the appropriately titled *The Arizona Cowboy* (1950) at a time when the cycle had almost come to a halt. Nevertheless he continued his western connections by starring in the 1958 Frontier Doctor television series as well as providing narrations for several Walt Disney productions. On the recording front he received a high country-chart placing with *Crying In The Chapel* (1953) and came up with a country-pop crossover hit in *Don't Go Near The Indians* (1962). The traditions were carried on by his son Rex Allen Jr who, after scoring some twenty chart hits in the 1970s, tried a short-lived bid at reviving western memories with *Can You Hear Those Pioneers* (1976) and *Last Of The Silver Screen Cowboys* (1982), the latter also featuring the voices of his father and Roy Rogers.

But, by the 1950s, the heyday of the singing cowboy had passed. The movies were demanding more realism, the Saturday matinees becoming part of a bygone era and the last of the studios handling such productions, Republic, were closing down their theatrical operations and moving into television. Western songs were fast going out of fashion, only to be heard as something different from the norm, like Marty Robbins telling the stories of *El Paso* (1959) and *Big Iron* (1960), or the accompanying theme song to a big-budget Hollywood production. There were odd instances of actors putting their voice on record, and achieving chart hits, like veteran Walter Brennan recalling *Old Rivers* (1962) or Bonanza's Lorne Green recounting the tale of *Ringo* (1964).

Likewise there was a similar demise for western swing, hurried on by the merging of honky tonk into country and the change of musical tastes in general. Bob Wills continued to record on a regular basis although, after his early-1960s sessions for Liberty Records (which reunited him with singer Tommy Duncan), he retired from working with the Texas Playboys through ill health and the latter-day recordings for Kapp (1965-69) were made with Nashville session musicians. He was elected into the Country Music Hall of Fame in 1968.

***Above:* After his boom period, Hank Thompson carried on the western-swing traditions, albeit in a more country setting. Over his long career as a singer he has achieved great success as a recording artist and has produced several big hits. His Brazos Valley Boys band was the top western band for 13 years running.**

The singer who carried on the western swing traditions, albeit in a more country presentation, was Hank Thompson (born Waco, Texas, 3 September 1925). His band, The Brazos Valley Boys, were named America's Number One Western Band for thirteen consecutive years (1953-65). A staunch fan of the Grand Ole Opry and western movies, he performed as 'Hank the Hired Hand' on radio station WACO in 1942. A little later, he was introduced to Capitol Records by Tex Ritter, which led to an eighteen-year association and millions of sales with distinctive hits like *Whoa Sailor* (1949), *The Wild Side Of Life* (1952), *Wake Up Irene* (1953) *The New Green Light* (1954), *Blackboard Of My Heart* (1956) and *Squaws Along The Yukon* (1958). Among Thompson's many achievements, he was the first country artist ever to play Las Vegas, at the Golden Nugget, and it's stated that he was the first country singer to record in hi-fi, to cut a stereo album and make a live country recording. He's continued to record over the years (for Warner Bros., Dot, MCA and Churchill) – and got back into the Top 10 with singles like *Smokey The Bar* (1968) and *The Older The Violin, The Sweeter The Music* (1974) – as well as keeping up stage appearances. He also maintains business operations out of Tulsa, Oklahoma, with country-music entrepreneur Jim Halsey (his manager since 1951) and entertainer Roy Clark.

A slight revival of western swing occured in the early 1970s, no doubt helped by musical historian Merle Haggard recording the album *A Tribute To The Best Damn Fiddle Player In The World (or, My Salute To Bob Wills)* in which the singer's band, The Strangers, combined with the talents of a number of one-time Texas Playboys including Eldon Shamblin, Tiny Moore, Alex Brashear, Johnny Gimble and Johnny Lee Wills. Some four years later Haggard once again rounded up members of the Playboys, this time with their long-time leader Bob Wills, to embark on an ambitious project that would eventually see the light of day as a boxed album set titled *For The Last Time.* Sadly Wills was only to be heard on a few of the tracks for, after the first day's recording, he suffered a heart attack and slipped into a coma. He never recovered, dying seventeen months later on 13 May 1975.

The western-swing movement has continued, albeit in a minor fashion. However, its popularity remains unchallenged in places like Texas and Oklahoma. Several members of the Texas Playboys re-formed for limited dates under the direction of Leon McAuliffe, and another one-time member of the band, Leon Rausch, keeps busy heading his own outfit, The Texas Panthers. The music wasn't to be overlooked by the younger musicians, with groups like Asleep At The Wheel and Alvin Crow and his Pleasant Valley Boys bringing the sounds to a whole new generation of record buyers. But, to the majority of people, the western aspect of country music is far more obvious these days . . . witnessed by the boots and stetsons adopted as essential clothing by many of the music's contemporary entertainers.

The Hank Williams Era

The war years changed the face of country music. It brought people of the various regional areas together, and cultures were exchanged as Northerners fought side by side with Southerners to combat a common enemy. Rural families were also uprooted to urban surroundings to work in industrial factories and munition plants. Out of the turmoil of change, country music suddenly became a reality to many who previously had witnessed it only on radio and records. Suddenly it had become a living music and, more importantly, it was discovered that the people whose music it was weren't hicks or hillbillies, as generally supposed.

It didn't just stop there. As servicemen went overseas, so their music went with them. Tours by country music stars became frequent and many servicemen started singing the music themselves to the accompaniment of a guitar. Others gathered together to form bands. At the same time country was frequently aired by the military broadcasting services, ensuring that the sounds were not only heard by the military but also by hundreds of thousands of civilians. A report in Billboard magazine during 1943 revealed that there were at least '25 hillbilly bands to be found within the European Theater of Operations' and indicated that country was 'the most popular form of music within the services.'

Some of the biggest hits of the war years were country songs. Ernest Tubb and Roy Acuff provided early successes with *Walking The Floor Over You* and *The Wreck On The Highway* respectively. In 1943 Al Dexter came up with one of the biggest sellers of the decade with *Pistol Packin' Mama* (moving one-and-a-half-million copies during its first year of release and encouraging Bing Crosby to record a pop version, just as he had done earlier with the country songs *San Antonio Rose* and *You Are My Sunshine*), and Ted Daffan changed status from successful songwriter to successful recording artist with *Born To Lose*. Then, in the year that hostilities ceased, Dexter was back with *Guitar Polka*, Jack Guthrie scored with *Oklahoma Hills* (penned by brother Woody) and Spade Cooley came into the spotlight with *Shame On You*. But the most spectacular success of them all was one that appealed directly to the spirit of the nation – Elton Britt's patriotic *There's A Star Spangled Banner Waving Somewhere* (1942), which quickly became a million seller and paved the way for a proliferation of war songs that included *The Soldier's Last Letter* (Ernest Tubb), *At Mail Call*

Above: **Ernest Tubb began his career on the radio in Texas in 1932 and in 1965 was made a member of the Country Music Hall of Fame. He now owns the world-famous Ernest Tubb Record Shops in Nashville.**
Right: **'When you get right down to it, he's still the most wanted outlaw in the land,' sing Hank Jr. and Waylon Jennings of Hank Williams Sr.**

Below: Hank Williams was a loner and an 'outlaw' 20 years before the word came into use to describe these geniuses of country music who just didn't fit the established mold. It was a fast life he lived, filled with both cheatin' hearts and cheated hearts, with honky-tonk blues at the end of the road. He wrote and recorded a fantastic wealth of country classics between the fall of 1949 and the fall of 1952 and before he took that last ride on New Year's Day, 1953.

Left: **Ralph Peer started his career as recording director of Okeh Records and established himself, very successfully, as a talent scout.** *Below:* **Studio A in Nashville, the famous studio where many of country music's greatest hits were recorded.**

Today (Gene Autry) and *Stars And Stripes On Iwo Jima* (Bob Wills).

As the war ended it was obvious that country music appealed to vast new audiences. The shifting of population during preceeding years ensured that the music's original rural concept now belonged to the past, and its fast-growing popularity was assured by the advance of communications as well as movies and jukeboxes. Greater commercialism drifted into the picture as industry offices in New York and Los Angeles suddenly realized that country's appeal was far greater than originally envisaged, a factor that wasn't overlooked by many of the artists themselves who saw the benefits (not least of all, financial) to be derived from big-selling hit records.

The most immediate effect of the changes was that Nashville started to develop as an industry center, although the movement at first was slow. Wesley Rose, president of Acuff-Rose Publications, was one person there at the start. he recalls:

When I first visited Nashville in 1943, Roy Acuff and my father (Fred Rose) has just started the music publishing company and that was the only thing in town connected with the music industry – apart from the Grand Ole Opry. There were no record companies, no other publishing companies, no booking agencies. In fact the Grand Ole Opry, or WSM, booked their own talent because there was no one else around. When I eventually settled in town in 1945, I used to have to make frequent trips to New York and Los Angeles in order that the record companies could hear our songs because there was no one in Nashville I could take them to. In some ways it was kind of lonesome there.

Fred Rose (born St Louis, Missouri, 24 August 1897) didn't start out in country though. An ambitious songwriting pianist, he had written pop hits (including *Deed I Do* and *Honest And Truly*) and was playing with Paul Whiteman's band by his mid-twenties. A meeting with Gene Autry led him to Hollywood and the creation of songs like *Be Honest With Me* (nominated for an Academy award) and *Tweedle-O-Twill*. In 1942 he moved to Nashville – a town that he had visited several years earlier – and went into the music-publishing business with Roy Acuff. At first the company was small and consisted entirely of Pee Wee King, Jenny Lou Carson, two or three artists from the Opry and Rose (who also penned under the name of Floyd Jenkins) and Acuff themselves. A few years later it made gigantic strides when Hank Williams contributed his writing efforts and, during the 1950s, was the most successful of all publishing companies with songs from such as Felice and Boudleaux Bryant, John D Loudermilk, Roy Orbison, the Everly Brothers, Marty Robbins and many others.

Besides scoring in country-music circles, Acuff-Rose also sought success in the pop field. Wesley Rose says:

I was told that pop acts didn't record country songs, but I was from Chicago and I was a pop man during the first years of my life. When I liked a song, coming from Chicago, I couldn't understand why somebody else in Chicago, or Detroit, or St. Louis shouldn't like it either. I wasn't a musician, so I wasn't getting carried away with chords or anything else technical. I think the man who was responsible for changing things was Mitch Miller (then working at Columbia) because he was responsible for getting so many country songs cut by pop artists – like *Cold Cold Heart* by Tony Bennett, *Hey Good Lookin'* by Frankie Laine, *Half As Much* by Rosemary Clooney, which also brought on *Tennessee Waltz* by Patti Page – and this, all of a sudden, gained a new importance for Nashville. I think that's how Nashville got started.

Other music publishers moved into country. A major boost was the creation of Hill Music and Range Music (later to merge as Hill and Range) in 1945 by Julian Aberbach who prophesied that the time was ripe for a hillbilly boom, and started handling songs by such as Bob Wills, Bill Monroe and Hank Snow. Southern Music – the oldest music-publishing company with country songs, established in New York in 1927 by pioneering talent-scout Ralph Peer – quickly followed suit with a Nashville office, as did Cedarwood and Tree.

Above: **Bill Boyd and his band of Cowboy Ramblers in the WRR studio. They helped make Victor a success in the 1930s.**

Above: Another of country music's big hit makers, Carl Smith scored around three dozen hits in the 1950s and made a number of movie appearances. Now he's basically retired on his ranch in Tennessee.
Above right and right: Although he faded away from the United States scene for several years, Slim Whitman regenerated his chart status through his success in the British Isles.
Below: Aaron Young sings *This Little Girl of Mine* to a young devotee. He was one of the hottest acts of the postwar years, with 20 hits in eight years by 1960.

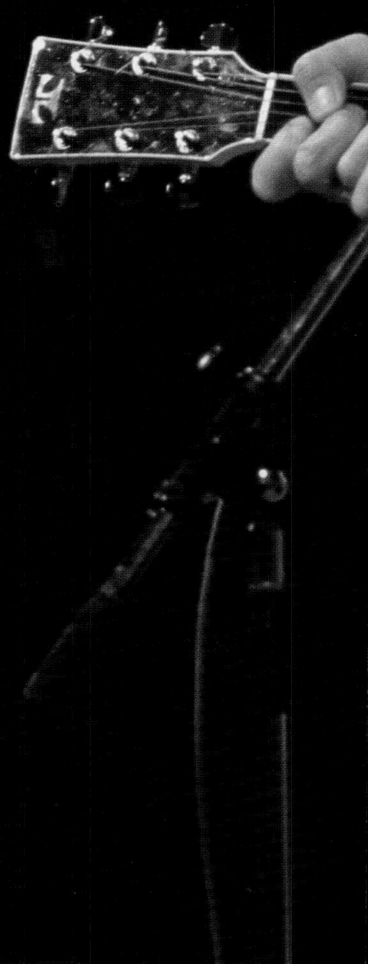

Next the record companies started viewing Nashville more seriously. Victor, which has been purchased by RCA (Radio Corporation of America) in 1929 and had built upon its early success by securing the talents of the Sons Of The Pioneers, Bill Monroe, Elton Britt, Ernest Tubb and Bill Boyd & the Cowboy Ramblers during the 1930s, signed the first of the postwar superstars in 1944. His name was Eddy Arnold (born Henderson, Tennessee, 15 May 1918), the son of an old-time fiddle player. He had built up his reputation as one of the most popular singers in East Tennessee through regular appearances on the Knoxville radio station, WTIS. Then came his Opry appearances as a member of Pee Wee King's Golden West Cowboys and the solo breakthrough.

His first releases on Victor came in 1947 and were *I'll Hold You In My Heart, It's A Sin* and *What Is Life Without Love* and, by the year's end, 2,700,000 records had been sold. For the next six years he virtually dominated the country scene and scored Number 1 records with *Don't Rob Another Man's Castle* (1949), *I'm Throwing Rice* (1949), *There's Been A Change In Me* (1951), *Kentucky Waltz* (1951), *Easy On The Eyes* (1952) and *Eddy's Song* (1953). He was a smooth crooner whose styling was perfectly complemented by the 'tingling' steel guitar sounds of 'Little' Roy Wiggins and provided a fine alternative to the emergence of honky tonk into country's mainstream. Such presentation, alongside the fast-growing list of hits, opened up major doorways to the movies and television, as well as attracting attention from the pop-record buyers. These ingredients, along with his own adaptability, saw him make a deliberate move to grab larger audience attention in the 1960s when, backed with 'Nashville Sound' production, he scored million sellers with such as *What's He Doing In My World* and *Make The World Go Away*, both released in 1965. By that time a number of the old-timers had decided that Arnold had long since deserted the country scene – in spite of his records continually scoring in the country charts – as his recordings comprised full string arrangements and he was frequently seen on stage attired in evening suit and accompanied by a full orchestra.

Nevertheless Eddy Arnold has remained a top leaguer and still ranks as one of the world's all-time record sellers, irrespective of categorization. Countrywise he's scored more 120 chart entries and, justly, he's a member of the Country Music Hall of Fame, gaining entrance in 1966, with a plaque that includes the inscription '. . . he was a powerful influence in setting musical trends.'

At the end of the war the Grand Ole Opry was the top country radio show and many of its performers were hit makers. It represented a wide cross section of country, with Ernest Tubb bringing in the sounds of honky tonk, Roy Acuff continuing traditions, Bill

Above: **The nationally popular Cowboy Copas *(second from right)* appeared at the Grand Ole Opry after World War II.**
Below: **Eddy Arnold first appeared at the Grand Ole Opry as a member of Pee Wee King's Golden West Cowboys, but quickly found solo success, with over 120 entries in the country charts.**

Right and below: Eddy Arnold was made a member of the Country Music Hall of Fame in 1966, having achieved all-time record sales worldwide.

Left: **Red Foley was the first country singer to have his own national radio show in 1939. He was elected to the Hall of Fame in 1967.**

Monroe presenting bluegrass and Zeke Clements, 'the Alabama Cowboy,' letting the nation know about western swing. Then the western image made its debut with the signing of Oklahoma's Cowboy Copas, a former member of WLW's Midwestern Jamboree who had just risen to nationwide popularity of the strength of a wartime hit *Filipino Baby*, and joined as a sideman to Pee Wee King. He quickly followed up with another hit, *Sign Sealed And Delivered* and, with the release of *Tennessee Waltz* and *Kentucky Waltz*, he soon became known as the 'Waltz King of the Grand Ole Opry.' George Morgan was another important new Opry act, his arrival in 1948 coming on the heels of his million-selling *Candy Kisses* as the show sought out another smooth-styled crooner to take Arnold's place. Also made a member of the Opry cast that same year was 'Little' Jimmy Dickens, a fine singer of heart songs but best known for, and most successful with, novelty offerings like *A-Sleepin' At The Foot Of The Bed* (1950) and *May The Bird Of Paradise Fly Up Your Nose* (1965). Dickens is one of the most recent members of the Country Music Hall of Fame, gaining admission in 1983.

Another popular attraction was Red Foley (born Berea, Kentucky, 17 June 1910), who was elected to the Hall of Fame in 1967 and described as 'one of the most versatile and moving performers of all time.' He came to the Opry by way of Chicago's National Barn Dance and the Renfro Valley Barn Dance (which he originated with John Lair), though he had already found fame by being the first country singer to have his own national radio show, Avalon Time (1939), which co-starred comedian Red Skelton. That led on to a record deal with Decca and initial success with *Smoke On The Water* (1944). His popularity gained a further boost when WSM chose him to host another program in addition to his Opry appearances, the Prince Albert Show, which also put the focus on Nashville's developing industry, and by the end of the decade he was selling millions of records. His biggest record successes were *Tennessee Saturday Night* (1948), *Chattanooga Shoeshine Boy* (1950), *Birmingham Bounce* (1950), and *Midnight* (1952) as well as a number of duets with Ernest Tubb including the chart-topping *Goodnight Irene* (1952). Later he hosted the Ozark Jubilee television shows, and co-starred with Fess Parker in the 1962 ABC-TV series Mr. Smith Goes To Washington. He died on 18 September 1968 in Fort Wayne, Indiana, following appearances on a Grand Ole Opry roadshow, eleven months after his admission to the Country Music Hall of Fame.

The artist who was to make the biggest impact of them all, and bring country into its modern age, was Hank Williams, a singer/songwriter destined to become a legend. He cited Roy Acuff and Ernest Tubb as his greatest influences, and his own music represented a cross between hillbilly and honky tonk. Like Jimmie Rodgers, he died tragically young, though his death was hurried on by his lifestyle – a death, wrote Robert Shelton in the New York Times, 'due to too much living, too much sorrow, too much love, too much alcohol and drugs.' He was the first casualty of the honky tonk lifestyle he sang about so plaintively in his songs.

Within a span of some six years, and a catalog of some 125 songs, he broke down the 'specialist' qualities of country and brought it to the attention of the mass public. He was born Hiram Hank Williams (Mount Olive, Alabama, 17 September 1923), the son of poor rural folks, and had the strains of hillbilly music around him from his earliest days. He was taught hymns and Southern gospel music by his mother, Lilly, and learned guitar, blues rhythms, and street life from an old negro musician named Tee-Tot. By the age of twelve he had won first prize in a songwriting competition and, two years later, had formed his first band, The Drifting Cowboys, finding work on Montgomery radio station, WSFA. In the mid-1940s – after drifting through a number of occupations, including working on a medicine show, where he began his stormy courtship with Audrey Shepard, and working in the Mobile shipyards – he re-formed his band and, featuring 'Miss Audrey' as a singer, failed an audition with the Grand Ole Opry but had secured a writer's contract with Acuff-Rose Publications. Fred Rose had signed the writer of the strength of songs like *Six More Miles To The Graveyard* and *My Love For you (Has Turned To Hate)*; he was on the lookout for material for Molly O'day, a singer who had gained a reputation as 'the female Roy Acuff.' Wesley Rose continues the story:

> At that time neither Hank, nor us, had any thoughts about him recording. That came later when a fellow in New York named Middleman, who was starting up a new label called Sterling Records, called my father and asked if he could produce a couple of acts – a western act and a hillbilly act. The western act was easy, we had the Willis Brothers who were known as the Oklahoma Wranglers in those days, but we didn't have a hillbilly act. Then we got to listening to some of Hank's songs again and we heard that he could sing, so we called him up and asked if he wanted to make some records – not under contract but for a flat fee. He came in and we cut four sides at the WSM studios, using the Oklahoma Wranglers as backup musicians, but all the cuts sounded like Roy Acuff which wasn't that surprising as Hank idolized him.
>
> It wasn't until Sterling requested another session that we heard Hank in his own right. During that session he did a song called

Right: **Little Jimmy Dickens became famous for such novelty songs as *May the Bird of Paradise Fly up You Nose.***

> *Honky Tonkin'* and there was no way that he could do that in an Acuff style because Acuff didn't do honky tonk songs. So, all of a sudden, we heard Hank Williams singing for the first time and that was when we decided to put him on a major label.

A deal was struck with the brand-new MGM Records (founded by former-Columbia executive Frank Walker, with Williams as first signing) and, around the same time, the singer made his debut on the Louisiana Hayride. Some two years later, as *Lovesick Blues* (ironically, not a Williams original but a 1920s song penned by Irving Mills and Charles Friend) was holding down a 42-week run in the charts, he made his never-to-be-forgotten first appearance on the Grand Ole Opry. A standing ovation greeted him, he sang (of course) *Lovesick Blues*, and he encored again . . . and again . . . in fact, six times in all and, so the story goes, the applause carried on for five minutes after he finally left the stage and returned to his dressing room. Naturally he became an Opry cast member, although some of the show's executives expressed anxiety about his lifestyle, including his drinking habits and his tendency to miss dates.

Within a year he was a major attraction in country music, earning top touring rates and ruling the charts with songs like *Long Gone Lonesome Blues* (1950), *Why Don't You Love Me* (1950), *Moaning The Blues* (1950) and *Cold Cold Heart* (1951), with the last named opening the gates to the pop market as Tony Bennett recorded a pop version and gathered over a million sales. Soon other pop artists started looking for a Williams' song and the snowball began rolling. Williams was never to realize his full success, his life started going downhill fast. The stormy relationship with his wife Audrey ended in divorce and a heavy settlement; he started adding pills and drugs (taken, originally, to counteract the pain from a spinal injury) to a steady diet of booze; began missing gigs regularly and was fired from the Opry. On 1 January 1953, in the back seat of his Cadillac, 200 miles outside of Knoxville, Tennessee, en route to a concert in Canton, Ohio, Hank Williams died. He was 29 years old and the whole world mourned the passing of its hillbilly bard.

Eight years later, when the Country Music Hall of Fame first opened its doorways, Hank Williams was the first in its hallowed hallways, alongside his mentor Fred Rose and the other pioneering father-figure Jimmie Rodgers. His plaque says it all:

> Performing artist, songwriter . . . Hank Williams will live on in the memories of Americans. The simple, beautiful melodies and straightforward, plaintive stories in his lyrics, of life as he knew it, will never die. His songs appealed not only to the country music field, but brought him great acclaim in the 'pop' music world as well.

Two decades later the message still rings true as his recordings continue to be reissued time and time again while artists like Charley Pride, Linda Ronstadt, The Carpenters, Ray Price and Moe Bandy ride to success on the back of a Williams' song.

By the time that Williams was turning out hit singles, the record companies were looking toward Nashville as a permanent recording base. RCA Victor had already recorded Eddy Arnold there in December 1944, making use of a makeshift WSM studio (and, earlier, had produced the first-ever Nashville recordings back in 1928 when, using portable equipment, it had recorded a number of Opry acts including DeFord Bailey and the Crook Brothers) though it was the independent Bullet label, owned by former Opry announcer Jim Bulleit, that secured the honor of making the first proper studio recording. It was made by Sheb Wooley – later to record the million-selling *Purple People Eater* (1958) and adopt the alter ego Ben Calder – in a disused WSM studio especially constructed by engineers George Reynolds, Carl Jenkins and Aaron Shelton. In 1947 these same engineers then opened up the famed Castle Studios, situated in the downtown Tulane Hotel, which was used by virtually every record label for several years.

But it was Owen and Harold Bradley who firmly established the recording business in town. The brothers had opened their first studio, the Bradley Film and Recording Studio, as early as 1952 and, a year later, moved to a new site in Nashville's Hillsboro Village area. Finally they built the reknowned 'Quonset Hut' studio (which Columbia Records later bought) on 16th Avenue South and the recording boom was on. Owen Bradley then secured a top niche with Decca Records and set about producing the label's artists, while his younger brother moved on to become one of Nashville's busiest session musicians.

As Nashville began to develop as country music's Mecca, new stars began to emerge. Webb Pierce (born West Monroe, Louisiana, 8 August 1926) was among the most successful and from 1952 – when he made his chart debut with *Wondering* – to 1960, he scored 32 hits, most of them going right to the top of the ladder. The first major step in his career came with appearances on his home state's Louisiana Hayride (with his first records coming out on the independent Four Star label), but once signed to Decca and moving on to the Opry, he quickly established himself as a leader in his field. His biggest hits centered around slippin' around (*Back Street Affair*, 1952) and drinkin' (*There Stands The Glass*, 1952, one of the best barroom songs ever) themes, all given that

Above left: **Lefty Frizzell had a distinctive drawling singing voice.**
Above: **Ferlin Husky started out as a radio deejay.**
Above right: **George Jones' songs appeal to a broad range of music listeners.**

rich, nasal styling that was to be the singer's distinctive trademark but, equally, was to prove unfashionable in later years. Among his other big hits were *It's Been So Long* (1953), *Slowly* (1954), *More And More* (1954), *I Don't Care* (1955) and a revival of Jimmie Rodgers' *In The Jailhouse Now* (1955). His sales totaled millions, and he also provided a guiding for others on their way up like Faron Young, Goldie Hill, steel guitarist Jimmy Day and pianist Floyd Cramer. Just for the record, he's the star who owns that guitar-shaped swimming pool in Nashville.

A close compatriot of Pierce's, and fellow member of the Louisiana Hayride before they joined the Grand Ole Opry, was Faron Young (born Shreveport, Louisiana, 25 February 1932). Their voices were entirely different though, with Young being more of a crooner which gave him an opening to the pop market on a couple of occasions with *Hello Walls* (1961) and *It's Four In The Morning* (1971, which took him right to the top of the British charts as well as achieving success in other overseas countries). Originally signed to Capitol, Young quickly became one of the hottest acts of the postwar years. By 1960 he had achieved 20 hits during an eight-year period, with *Goin' Steady* (1953), *Live Fast, Love Hard And Die Young* (1955), *Alone With You* (1958) and *Country Girl* (1959) among his other well-known songs. He also kept busy with touring and television work, and made a number of movies, including *Country Music Holiday* (1958) with Zsa Zsa Gabor and Ferlin Husky. He was, and still is, one of the music's most colorful characters, never afraid to speak his mind and always ready to help others. Kris Kristofferson and Charley Pride were just a couple who benefited from Young's assistance.

The career of Ferlin Husky (born Flat River, Missouri, 3 December 1927) might well have suffered from an identity crisis, for he began his professional career as a deejay in Bakersfield, California, working under the name of Terry Preston (a title that he also used for concert performances and early recordings) as well as introducing a hayseed character into his act named Simon Crum. But it was a tribute record to Hank Williams, *Hank's Song* (1953), recorded under the Husky name that gave him the initial break, so Preston 'retired' though Crum remained (and achieved a smash hit in 1958 with *Country Music Is Here To Stay*). His other early success was a chart-topping duet with Jean Shepard *Dear John Letter* (1953) – which evolved a sequal that same year, *Forgive Me John* – and from 1955 he became a regular contributor to the charts, notching up over 30 hits during the following fifteen years. He was also one of the first country singers to make a pop-chart breakthrough, with *(Since You've) Gone* (1957) and repeated it later with the religious *Wings Of A Dove* (1960).

Another big 1950s hitmaker was Carl Smith (born Maynardsville, Tennessee, 15 March 1927) who, on the Columbia label, chalked up 34 chart successes before the decade was out. He commenced his career after a stint in the Navy, and after gaining popularity through appearances on radio stations in Georgia and North Carolina, came back to his home state and joined the Opry in May 1950. A little over a year later his second single, *Let's Live A Little,* made the charts while his fourth, *Let Old Mother Nature Have Her Way* (1951), went to the top. He then followed up with such as *Don't Just Stand There* (1952), *Hey Joe* (1953), *Loose Talk* (1954) and *Kisses Don't Lie* (1955). From there on he expanded his activities into other medium areas, which included movies – *The Badge Of Marshall Brennan* (1957) and *Buffalo Guns* (1962) – and hosting his own long-running television series in Canada. Wtih some fifteen million sales during his fifteen-year

association with Columbia, he moved on to Acuff-Rose's Hickory label but, these days, he's basically retired on his 600-acre ranch on the outskirts of Nashville.

Of course Texas continued to keep the country scene supplied with outstanding talent, and among the most popular were Lefty Frizzell, George Jones and Ray Price. All could be classed as influential honky-tonk singers, though Price – like Eddy Arnold – was to change his music dramatically over the years.

A highly distinctive vocal stylist, William Orville Frizzell (born Corsiana, Texas, 31 March 1928) – nicknamed 'Lefty,' following a short career as a boxer – started out among the dance halls and radio stations of West Texas and New Mexico before a demo tape got him a record deal with Columbia. The song *if You've Got The Money, I've Got The Time* took him to the top of the charts in late 1950, and soon established itself as a country classic. The following year the singer set more records; *I Want To Be With You Always, Always Late, Mom And Dad's Waltz* and *Travelin' Blues* were all in the Top 10 at the same time. Among other famed recordings were *Long Black Veil* (1959) and *Saginaw, Michigan* (1964) and, all in all, he chalked up around 30 hits during his 22-year association with the label. It wasn't just the hits or his songwriting abilities that made him a legend; rather it was his distinctive, drawling phrasing and rich voice which provided a subtlety to his lyrics that was to influence latterday singers like Willie Nelson, Merle Haggard and Johnny Rodriguez. Success, however, brought its pitfalls and, throughout his career, Frizzell fought a serious drink problem that could have contributed to his death at the age of 47 in 1975. Seven years later he was elected into the Country Music Hall of Fame. Today the Frizzell name is carried on by his younger brothers David and Allan, and two years after his death, Nelson cut a loving tribute album, *To Lefty From Willie*.

Equally distinctive, though with an entirely different styling is George Jones (born Saratoga, Texas, 12 September 1931), a singer of the grand honky-tonk tradition who has remained a top leaguer for almost 30 years in spite of numerous personal problems that have included drinking, drugs, bankruptcies and broken marriages, one of them to Tammy Wynette. The possessor of an incredible vocal range, Jones frequently has been cited as 'a singer's singer' and his appeal stretches across the board from country to rock. (British rockers Dave Edmunds and Elvis Costello both name him as an important influence, with Edmunds scoring a pop hit with Jones' *The Race Is On* in 1982 and Costello duetting with him on *A Stranger In The House* a couple of years earlier.)

Born into a nonprofessional, musical family, Jones' first influences were Ernest Tubb and songwriter Floyd Tillman (and, later, Hank Williams), and he began his career after serving in the Marines. He made his recording debut on Starday, a new independent label formed by H W 'Pappy' Daily and Jack Starnes in Beaumont, Texas, instantly scoring a Top 5 hit with the self penned *Why Baby Why* (1955). The artist-producer relationship of Jones and Daily was to prove one of the most successful and lasting in modern country-music history, stretching over four different labels in sixteen years, with the brief Starday debut leading on to Mercury, United Artists and, from 1965-71, Daily's own label, Musicor. The hits were numerous, amounting to more than 70 during this period and including the Number 1s *White Lightning* (1959), *Tender Years* (1961), *She Thinks I Still Care* (1962) and *Walk Through This World With Me* (1967). In addition he cuts duets with Melba Montgomery, resulting in the classic *We Must Have Been Out Of Our Minds* (1963), Margie Singleton, Brenda Carter and Gene Pitney among others.

In 1971 he severed the Daily connection and signed a recording deal with Epic, leading to his productions being handled by Billy Sherrill, one of Nashville's leading exponants of the smooth,

Right: **George Jones is among the most influential of all modern-day singers, and his music blares forth from bars like the Palace Tavern *(bottom).***
Below: **Ray Price changed the sound of country music.**

country-pop sound. But, even if some of the subsequent recordings were laden with string sections, nothing could hide his authentic voice and unique styling, and he remained at the top with songs such as *The Grand Tour* (1974) and *The Door* (1974) as well as a series of duets with Tammy Wynette including *We're Gonna Hold On* (1973), *Golden Ring* (1976) and *Near you* (1976). Then, in 1980, as his life had become more and more of a mess, and hardly ever out of the public eye, he proved that success can overcome all adversity – and came right back to the top with *He Stopped Loving Her Today* (penned by Curly Putman and Bobby Braddock and about – though never mentioned – another of the music's troubled heroes, Hank Williams). It was a million-selling success, crossed over into the pop charts and won CMA Awards in both 1980 and 1981, giving Jones, surprisingly, his first major accolades in a long career.

Dallas' Big D Jamboree provided an early stepping stone for Ray Price (born Perryville, Texas, 12 January 1926), an artist who has not only kept up with trends over the years but frequently set them himself. First recording for the small Bullet label (*Jealous Lies,* 1950), he moved into the major league with a Columbia deal and the single *Talk To Your Heart* (1952). He scored his first million seller with *Crazy Arms* (1956) and his second with *City Lights* (1958), and other big hits of the period include *Release Me* (1954), *My Shoes Keep Walking Back To You* (1957) and *Heartaches By The Number* (1959).

Price was known as 'the Cherokee Cowboy,' with his first band being The Cherokee Cowboys made up from members of Hank Williams' Drifting Cowboys, and his music cut between the plaintiveness of Williams' lyrics and the honky-tonk swing sound of his regional upbringing. But he was able to foretell changes and his success allowed him to ring them. 'Actually, in 1954, I came up with

Above: **Ray Price's innovations brought him great success.**
Left: **Johnny Wright and the Harmony Girls, Louise and Muriel. In 1943 Johnny changed Muriel's stage name to Kitty Wells and she became 'Queen of Country Music.'**
Below right: **Buddy Emmons is received into the Steel Guitar Hall of Fame.**

the basic country sound that's now well familiar. Up to that time it was 2/4 bass and no drums,' Price explains. 'Of course Bob Wills used drums but his was a dance band. They didn't have them in country bands, and certainly not on the Grand Ole Opry. But I forced them finally to let me have them.'

He also slipped string arrangements into some recordings – *Make The World Go Away* (1963) and *Burning Memories* (1964) and, in 1967, went the whole way with 47 pieces being used on *Danny Boy*. At first deejays boycotted him (and some even refused to play a Ray Price record for three years), but it didn't stop it getting into the Top 10. The strings stuck and in 1970 he recorded Kris Kristofferson's *For The Good Times*. It was another Number 1 and broke into the pop market, while the album remained in the charts for some four years and gathered sales of several million.

Price accounts his success to 'wanting to be in the majority. Originally country was a specialist music and in the minority, but I didn't want to be there. It had to broaden its base if it were to be

Below (left to right): **Johnny and Jack, Kitty Wells and *(inset)* the Tennessee Mountain Boys – Emory Martin, Paul Warren and Ray Atkins – after a performance on the Louisiana Hayride in 1950.**

accepted like the way it is these days.' In recent times he's semi-retired and breeds horses on his Texas ranch, though he still continues to make occasional stage appearances and records. Historically he's one of country's most important contributors, not only for his innovative touches but also for providing initial breaks to such as Willie Nelson, Roger Miller, Johnny Bush (who's continued that old Price sound in his recordings), Johnny Paycheck and steel guitarists Buddy Emmons and Jimmy Day, all of whom played in Price's band at one time or another.

Across the Gulf of Mexico from Texas, Slim Whitman (born Tampa, Florida, 20 January 1924), another one-time member of the Louisiana Hayride, gave country music a different kind of song during the early 1950s. Recording for Imperial (a West Coast label that originally did a lot of recording in the Texas-Louisiana area, with western swing's Adolph Hofner being one of its first country acts), many of his great hits didn't stem from country sources at all but, rather, from pop and light-operatic realms – like *Indian Love Call* (1952), *Secret Love* (1954) and *Rose Marie* (1954). However *Cattle Call* (1955), reinforced by his powerful yodeling proved that he was equally at home with a western song. He also set the pace by becoming the first country artist to build up an international reputation, especially in Britain where his *Rose Marie* topped the pop charts for eleven weeks (and set a record yet to be broken) and

Above: **Webb Pierce started out on the Louisiana Hayride and became a leader in his field in a short time.**
Right: **Kitty Wells and her husband, Johnny Wright, lead their own family show. She broke down the barriers against women in country and opened the door for others to follow.**

was the first country singer to appear at the world-famous London Palladium. It was Britain, in the 1970s, that was responsible for the Whitman revival, leading on to his *All My Best* gaining US television merchandizing and selling around one-and-a-half million units. From there he returned to touring and came under the wing of producer Pete Drake for recordings released on the Cleveland International label.

Possibly the most significant development in the early 1950s came with Kitty Wells' recording of *It Wasn't God Who Made Honky Tonk Angels* (1952), an 'answer song' to Hank Thompson's *Wild Side Of Life*. It rose to the top of the charts and broke down what seemed the male's territory. The female singer had arrived in country music. Of course there had been female singers before her, but most of these were associated with groups and were mostly connected with the music's more old-timey aspects. She broke down the barriers and, within a short while, was acknowledged as 'the Queen of Country Music.'

A native Nashvillean (born 30 August 1919), Wells began singing on local station WSIX in 1936 and, two years later, married Johnny Wright of the popular Johnny & Jack (Anglin) duo. She became a featured performer on their stage show, although achieving stardom was given a back seat to raising her three children, Ruby, Carol and Bobby. (All three, later, became a part of the Kitty Wells-Johnny Wright family show, with Bobby developing roads into Hollywood which included a four-year stint on the top-rating television series McHale's Navy.) Kitty appeared on the Louisiana Hayride during the years 1947-52, which led on to a 30-year association with Decca Records. *Honky Tonk Angels* was followed by another 'answer song,' *Paying For That Back Street Affair* (1953), the female viewpoint to the Webb Pierce song, and the decade continued with songs such as *Making Believe* (1955), *I Can't Stop Loving You* (1958) and *Mommy For A Day* (1959).

All in all Kitty Wells scored more than 70 chart successes, as well as numerous awards and accolades, including a citation as Outstanding Tennessee Citizen by Governor Frank Clement in 1954 and admission to the Country Music Hall of Fame in 1976. But her role in country music is indisputable and she opened the doorway to other female singers. Among the first to follow was Jean Shepard (born Pauls Valley, Oklahoma, 21 November 1933), a favorite with Grand Ole Opry audiences since 1955 and the possessor of a powerful voice. She originally started out as a member of an all-female western swing band, The Melody Ranch Girls, though her talent shone through enough to impress Hank Thompson and arrange an introduction for her with Capitol Records' Ken Nelson. A deal was clinched and she made her chart debut dueting with Ferlin Husky on *Dear John Letter* (1953), then making it on her own with songs that included *Satisfied Mind* (1955), *Beautiful Lies* (1955) and *Second Fiddle (To An Old Guitar)* (1964). After a slump in her fortunes, and a change of label to United Artists, she came back with a bang in 1973 with the Bill Anderson-penned *Slippin' Away*.

The 1950s saw country music going through a golden era, with the sounds of guitars and fiddles broadening the music's basic foundation and an ever-expanding roster of artists spreading the message to brand-new audiences. But the glories were to be relatively shortlived. Rock 'n' roll was on its way and country was never to sound the same again.

Rockabilly

At the same time that country was building its new roster of singers, the South was brewing up a new sound that would revolutionize the pop world. Popular music had its superstars like Frank Sinatra, Bing Crosby and newcomer Tony Bennett, as well as the big bands of Benny Goodman and Nelson Riddle, but they didn't satisfy the youth market now seeking a music that it could call its own. It was now looking toward the area of grassroots American music and, as well as seizing upon a number of the country recordings, was also viewing Negro music, once known as 'race' music but now more commonly titled rhythm 'n' blues.

During the late 1940s jukeboxes started featuring material by such as Muddy Waters and Howlin' Wolf, and several black recordings of the period, including Wynonie Harris' *Good Rockin' Tonight* and Fats Domino's *The Fat Man*, sold well across the board. Then radio made its pitch, with the first program to feature rhythm 'n' blues records being hosted by New York deejay Alan Freed. It was titled 'Moondog Rock 'n' Roll Party' and commenced its run in 1951.

Next came the country connection, though it had never been that far removed as, historically, the cultures had been thrown together in the South and the heavier beat of rhythm 'n' blues had already infiltrated itself into several top-selling country recordings. The Delmore Brothers and pianist Moon Mullican had pioneered country boogie, while Red Foley's *Tennessee Saturday Night* (1948) had a good rocking beat. Several of Hank Williams' records bore overtures to rock 'n' roll, as did a couple of 'Tennessee' Ernie Ford's big sellers, *Smokey Mountain Boogie* (1949) and *Shotgun Boogie* (1950).

Out of the fusion of the musics, which also included traces of western swing, grew a new sound and a new name came into the musical vocabulary, rockabilly, which quickly led on to the mainstream rock 'n' roll movement. Bill Haley set things ablaze with *Rock Around The Clock* (1955) although, beforehand, he had gained only regional success as a Country singer. During the late 1940s and early 1950s he had worked with a number of bands, including The Saddlemen (later renamed The Four Aces Of Western Swing), but first started gained attention when he recorded *Rocket 88*, a song penned by rhythm 'n' blues singer Jackie Brenston. Later, toward the end of his life, he made a move back to his country roots when he recorded a couple of Nashville-based albums for Sweden's Sonet Records.

Meanwhile things were happening in Memphis, Tennessee, as another white singer – with an obvious country and gospel background, and a liking for the black man's music – cut his first record. The singer was Elvis Presley, the label was Sun, and the single comprised *That's All Right Mama* (a 1946 blues song by Arthur 'Big

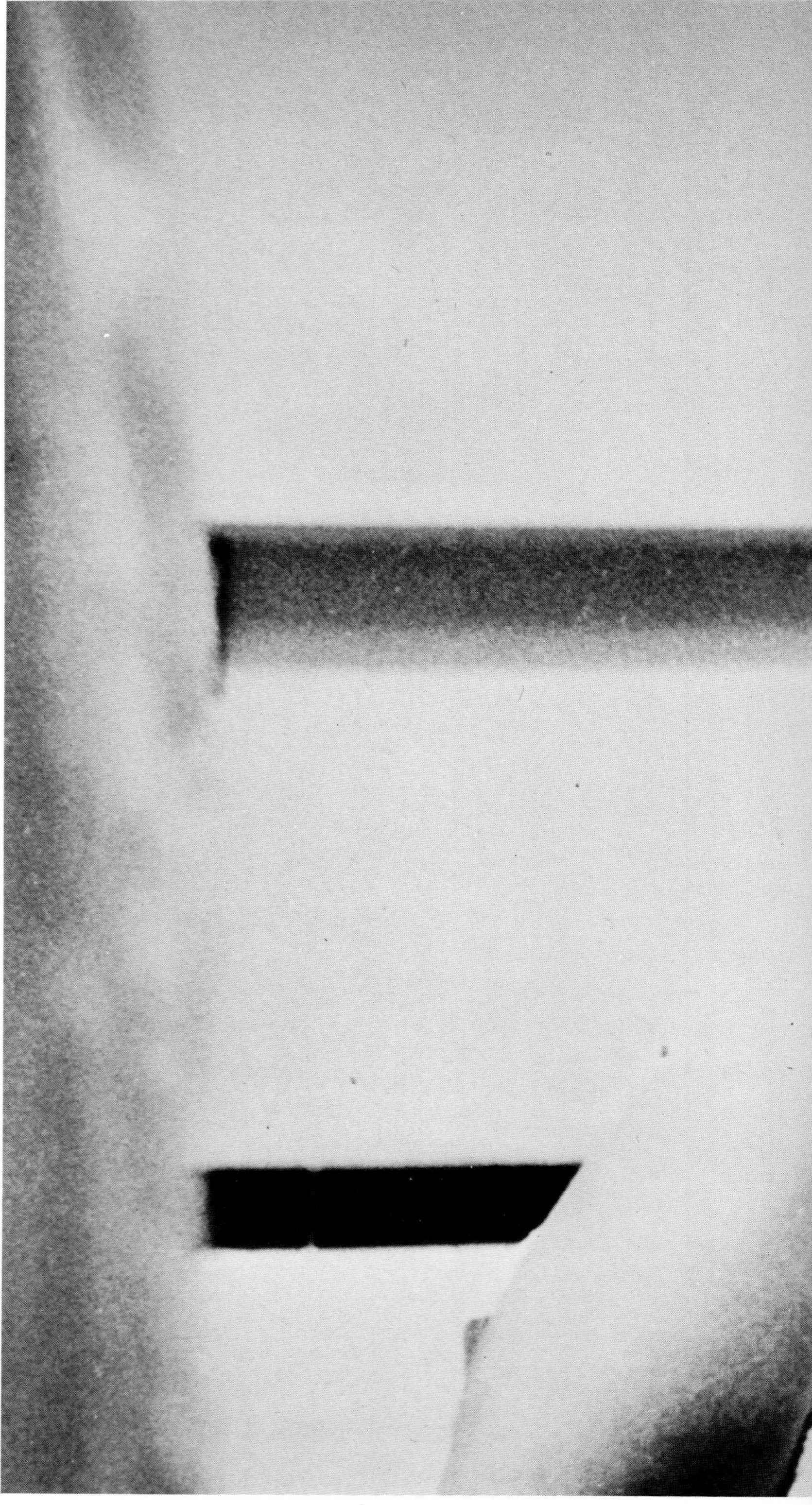

Right: **The young Elvis Presley made a successful appearance on the Louisiana Hayride as 'The Hillbilly Cat.'**

Boy' Crudup) and *Blue Moon Of Kentucky* (by bluegrass father Bill Monroe). The memorable recording date was 5 July 1954, though another year was to pass before the singer first gained entry into the country charts with *Baby Let's Play House*.

Millions of words have already been written about Elvis Presley (born Tupelo, Mississippi, 8 January 1935), and here only the singer's role within country realms will be discussed. The associaton with Sun had kicked off when the label's owner, Sam Phillips, was on the look out 'for a white man who possessed a Negro feel in his music' in the belief he could make a billion dollars out of such a deal. *That's All Right Mama* quickly established itself as the best-selling record in Memphis and, following the release of his second single (*Good Rockin' Tonight* and *I Don't Care If The Sun Don't Shine*), Presley guested on Hank Snow's portion of the Grand Ole Opry. The appearance was a failure, but it was an entirely different matter when he debuted on Shreveport's Louisiana Hayride. There ecstatic audience reaction ensured the singer, who was billed as 'The Hillbilly Cat' and performed with guitarist Scotty Moore and bassist Bill Black, received a year's contract. Next he started making road appearances with top name country singers, among them Hank Snow. With his fifth single, *Mystery Train* coupled with *I Forgot To Remember To Forget* (1955) he was at the top of the country charts and the major RCA deal was just around the corner. He still continued to turn out rockabilly records, but without the raw guts of his Sun efforts, the recordings now being made in Nashville with sessions musicians

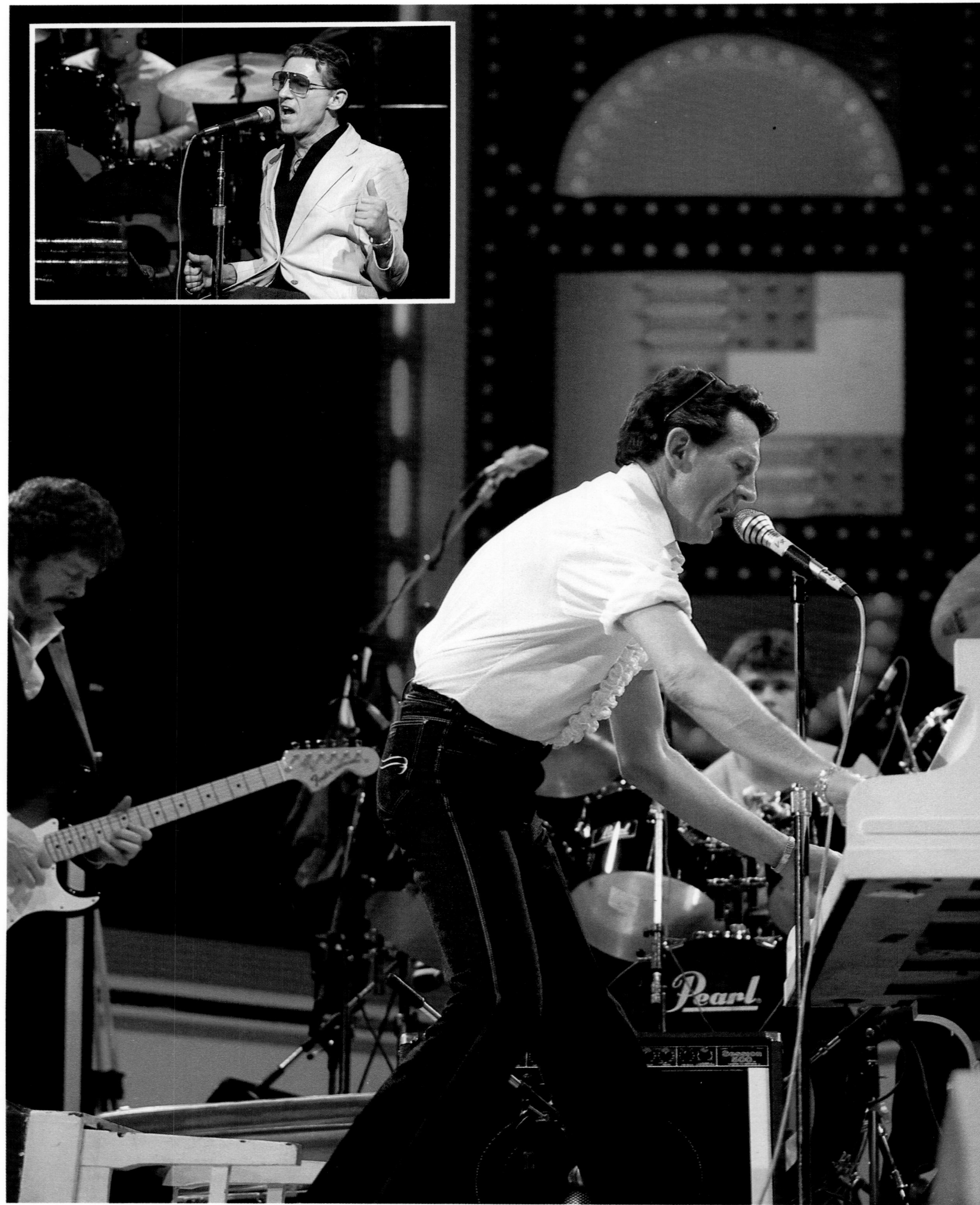
Pearl

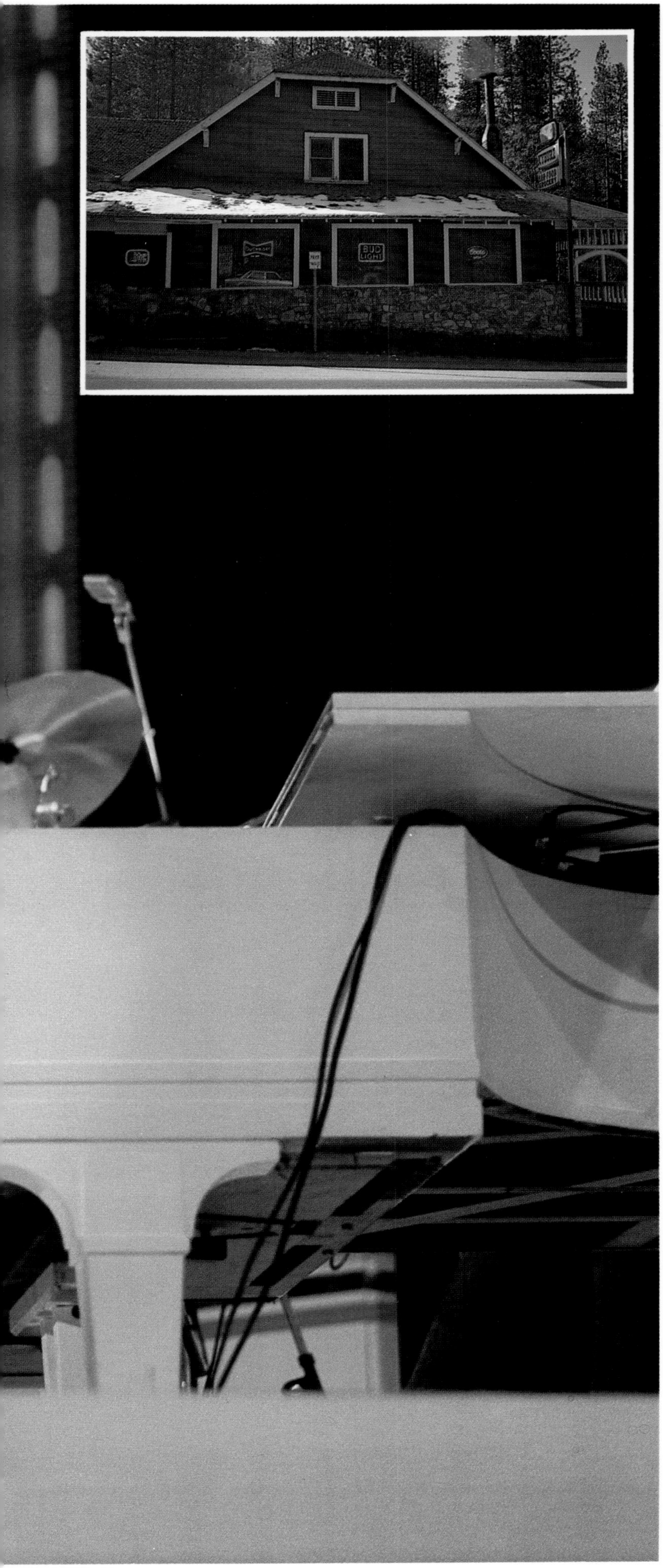

Left and inset far left: **Jerry Lee Lewis in full swing on stage. His performances are still as exuberant as ever.**
Above: **Elvis Presley and the Jordanaires made recordings and movie soundtracks together.**
Inset left: **A western roadhouse, typical of those where rockabilly was born.**

such as Chet Atkins, Floyd Cramer and the Jordanaires. He still continued to remain a firm fixture in the country charts, although he had also made a phenomenal crossover to the pop charts. Songs like *Heartbreak Hotel* (1956), *Teddy Bear* (1957) and *Jailhouse Rock* (1957) were all country best sellers and it was only after his time in the Army and the commencement of the movie career that his music started to move in an entirely different direction. Nevertheless he remained a firm favorite with numerous country fans, and many of his later recordings were penned by country writers. These included *U.S. Male* (1968, penned by Jerry Reed), *In The Ghetto* (1969, by Mac Davis), *Always On My Mind* (1972, by Johnny Christopher, Wayne Thompson and Mark James, and later to become a monster hit for Willie Nelson) and *Moody Blue* (1976, by Mark James). Clearly the country ties always remained firm.

The development of Elvis Presley didn't make Sam Phillips 'a billion' (the sale of the contract to RCA only netted him $40,000), but he was the catalyst for the most incredible grouping of dynamic talent ever to be seen on an independent label. Raised amidst the sound of the blues on a plantation in Florence, Alabama, this was the music that he first started recording in Memphis, working with artists like Bobby Bland and B B King. When he founded Sun in 1952 (and, later, associate labels Phillips International and Flip), he carried on recording black artists initially, though always on the look out for that 'white singer with a negro voice.' Besides Presley his major discoveries were Jerry Lee Lewis, Johnny Cash and Carl Perkins and he provided the launching pad for the careers of Charlie Rich, Roy Orbison and Conway Twitty.

Out of the three main contenders, Johnny Cash had the least to do with rockabilly and within three years of his first Sun single, *Cry, Cry, Cry* (1955), had signed a contract with Columbia where he moved on to become one of country's living legends. His contri-

Fender

Above and left: From gospel beginnings to rockabilly and on to country, Jerry Lee Lewis, shown dazzling British audiences, remains one of music's most extroverted entertainers.

Opposite page and above: **A masterful singer, songmaster and guitarist, Carl Perkins might have gone right to the top of the ladder were it not for a tragic automobile accident that kept him hospitalized for years during the mid-1950s.**
Above left: **Jerry Lee Lewis' pianos sometimes have to be very sturdy to withstand his energetic performances.**

butions to the music are discussed later but, for the present, merely let it be noted that Sun gave the public the first opportunity to hear that deep, gravelly voice and the distinctive back accompaniment of The Tennessee Two (guitarist Luther Perkins and bassist Marshall Grant), a sound that was to remain his trademark forever. He came to the label after hearing Presley and *Cry, Cry, Cry* (a song that he had written overnight upon Phillips' request for original material) opened the doorways. Six months later his famed *I Walk The Line* (1956) began a 42-week run in the charts, and he was topping them in 1958 with *Ballad Of A Teenage Queen*. Both these records, incidentally, made substantial inroads into the pop charts, thus assuring the singer of mass-audience appreciation.

Regarded by many as the definitive rockabilly artist, Carl Perkins (born Jackson, Tennessee, 9 April 1932) had gained initial recognition on Dallas' Big D Jamboree. He sent several demo tapes around to record companies in Nashville and New York before auditioning for Phillips, and his first single, *Movie Magg* (1955), came out on the Flip label. As was the producer's common policy, a country song was coupled with the rockabilly offering and, here, the artist presented a ballad, *Turn Around*. But it was the uptempo rockabilly side that caught the attention of the deejays and, fired by the artist's enthusiasm to continue with such tunes and using money from Presley's RCA contract, Sam Phillips decided to mount a major campaign around Perkins as the person to take Presley's place. Perkins, being a prolific songwriter, quickly came up with *Blue Suede Shoes* (1956) and the campaign was set in motion. The record turned out to be the record company's biggest commercial success, scoring over a million sales (in spite of a Presley cover version) and put the singer at the top of the country, pop and rhythm 'n' blues charts.

He followed up with *Boppin' The Blues* and *Dixie Fried*, both released in 1956, and when he looked set to become rockabilly's real superstar, tragedy struck in the form of an automobile accident, the results of which his brother Jay later died. By the time Carl had fully recovered, rockabilly had seen its boom period and after trying to reassert his position, he eventually returned to country music. For a number of years he toured with his Sun compatriot Johnny Cash, and recorded for a number of different labels including Dollie, Columbia and Mercury. Nevertheless his influence as a guitarist and songwriter has remained untarnished and has made itself felt to a whole later generation of rock musicians.

'The Killer,' Jerry Lee Lewis (born Ferriday, Louisiana, 29 September 1935) was the wild man of rockabilly, and the fall guy for the rock 'n' roll movement, confirming moralists' worst fears when he confessed that he 'was fourteen when he first married, and a bigamist at the age of sixteen.' Then came the scandal of his 1958 British tour when it was discovered that his then-current wife Myra (in fact, his third) was only thirteen and, to boot, his second cousin.

Above: **Carl Perkins displays his skills as both singer and guitarist.**
Left: **Conway Twitty, regarded by many as the definitive rockabilly artist, and Loretta Lynn, partners in the music business.**
Right: **Roy Orbison has a loose connection with country music but his hits brought attention to Nashville's recording scene.**

The tour was cancelled after three concerts and, back home in the USA, his career quickly fell to pieces, taking another ten years and a return to country music before he achieved a hit of any consequence. The song was *Another Time, Another Place* (1968), a somewhat philosophical title in the light of what had happened before.

Nevertheless his contributions to the music far override the scandals, although authority never looked upon him kindly, even from the early days when he retired from a likely preacher's career after his Bible Institute teachers frowned upon the way he bopped them old gospel songs. He played piano in the Moon Mullican tradition, but adding his own 'pumping' styling which eventually won him over to Sam Phillips. He made his chart debut with the double sided *Crazy Arms* (the Ray Price version was still selling at the time) and *End Of The Road* in 1956 and, within a year, had given Sun two more of its biggest successes, *Whole Lotta Shakin' Goin' On* and *Great Balls Of Fire*. *Breathless* (1958) came next but, by the time of *High School Confidential* (from the 1958 movie of the same name), the good times had just about rocked to an end.

Left, all four: **'Little Miss Dynamite,' Brenda Lee had made her chart debut at 13 and her string of pop successes added to Nashville's status as a recording center. She was one of the few women to make rockabilly hits.**
Above: **Patti Page became well known as a singer in the 1950s.**

In recent times Lewis has been one of country music's most consistent hit makers, averaging about three chart titles a year, and hitting the top with such as *To Make Love Sweeter For You* (1968), *Would You Take Another Chance On Me* (1971) and *Chantilly Lace/Let's Think About It Darling* (1972). But he doesn't seem to have quietened down much and often carries on his exuberant lifestyle on stage, where he still manages to create the frenzied excitement of bygone days.

By the early 1960s Sun Records had passed its peak and, though it continued to turn out rockabilly records by such as Charlie Rich, Carl Mann and Billy Lee Riley (as well as giving the first breaks for others like Dickey Lee, Ed Bruce, David Houston and Billy Swan), the label failed to register any significant success in the national charts. In 1968 Sun finally closed its doors and lay dormant for about a year until Shelby Singleton Jr. bought the entire catalog and set about a program of reissues through his SSS International operation. Previously Singleton had been with Mercury, and was responsible for bringing the Big Bopper, Johnny Preston and Bruce Channel to the label, before setting up his own independent company which hit paydirt in 1968 with Jeannie C Riley's multimillion-selling *Harper Valley PTA*.

The interest in Sun has continued, with the greatest enthusiasm stemming from Britain where, under a licensing deal with Charly Records and thanks to label historians Martin Hawkins and Colin Escott (authors of *Sun Records: The Brief Undiscovered History Of The Legendary Record Label*), a number of undiscovered treasures, and some duds, have seen the light of day alongside the reissues. The company has also delighted fans by issuing a three-album set from Carl Perkins, a five-album from Johnny Cash and a staggering twelve-album, 209-song set from Jerry Lee Lewis.

Left: Johnny Cash in 1970, a living legend with a very distinctive sound.
Below: Don *(left)* and Phil Everly scored a nonstop run of hits in the late 1950s and 1960s.

While Sun was a launching pad for a new generation of musicians, it didn't have the field entirely to itself. Others followed in the label's footprints, obviously enthralled by what they heard from the Memphis studios. One of these was Conway Twitty (born Harold Lloyd Jenkins, Friars Point, Mississippi, 1 September 1933), and destined to become a dominant force in both rock and country music.

In this instance there was no prior rhythm 'n' blues influence. He grew up listening to the records of Acuff and Tubb and, during his two years in the Army, formed a country band called The Cim-

This page: **The Everly Brothers appeared on British television in 1964 and, 19 years later, gave a Reunion Concert in London.**
Above right: **Wanda Jackson's shortlived association with Rockabilly took her to the top. These days she devotes her attention to gospel music.**

arrons. It was after hearing Presley's *Mystery Train* (1955) that he knew the musical direction he wanted to seek out, though his brief association with Sun proved unspectacular. (He recorded under the name of Harold Jenkins and his Rockhousers, but the results did not appear on the market until 1970.) Then he changed his name to Conway Twitty, signed a deal with MGM and quickly established himself as the label's heavyweight in the rock market, selling around sixteen-million records in five years. The biggest were *It's Only Make Believe* (1958) and *Mona Lisa* (1960), both of which accounted for over one-million sales. He also appeared on all the major television shows and made six movies, including *Platinum High, Sex Kittens Go To College* and *College Confidential*, writing the themes and soundtrack music for all of them. In 1966 Twitty returned to country music and commenced his Decca association with *Guess My Eyes Were Bigger Than My Heart*, setting the pace for a string of hits that would know few rivals. But that's another story, to be told later. . . .

Rockabilly wasn't just limited to one regional area, nor to one particular kind of sound. Lubbock, Texas, was the home of Buddy Holly, a singer who's childhood influences included Jimmie Rodgers and the Carter Family and whose first recordings, as demos, were made as a country artist, but the label later changed its mind as Holly's recordings were much gentler than others, and more closely related to pop music. Strangely Holly was the only

country-born, rockabilly star never to chart countrywise! Gene Vincent, from Norfolk, Virginia, fared slightly better, though his one country chart entry – *Be-Bob-A-Lula* (1956), co-penned by the singer and 'Sheriff' Tex Davis (later to become a well-respected and long-serving promotions man at Fred Foster's Monument Records in Nashville) – also proved to be the biggest hit of a short-lived career at Capitol. Originally intended as a 'B' side to *Woman Love,* it turned out a million seller and, technically, not that far removed from Presley's *Heartbreak Hotel* (1956) in its use of echo.

Like the country scene of a few years earlier, rockabilly was to be virtually male-only territory; Wanda Jackson and Brenda Lee were the only women to make chart impressions. In fact Wanda Jackson (born Maud, Oklahoma, 20 October 1937) is the only one who could be termed an out and out rocker. Brenda Lee's recordings – like Holly's – were closer to pop, though her powerful voice gave little indication of her diminutive size or tender years. Having gained her own radio show by the age of thirteen, Jackson made a country impression first by touring with Hank Thompson – and then was seen making concert appearances with Elvis Presley, leading to a dramatic change of style, a deal with Capitol and a rocking hit with *Let's Have A Party* (1960). However a year later she returned to country and commenced a run of some 30 chart appearances with *Right Or Wrong* and *In The Middle Of A Heartache.* These days she confines herself to gospel music.

Brenda Lee (born Augusta, Georgia, 11 December 1944), also started her career young living up to her title 'Little Miss Dynamite.' She was singing by the age of four and had progressed through numerous television shows before arriving on Red Foley's Ozark Jubilee, and receiving a Decca recording contract, before she reached her teens. After making her country chart debut with *One Step At A Time* (1957), with the aid of producer Owen Bradley she launched into a stream of rock and pop records that would add up to 29 successes in a seven-year period, among them *Sweet Nothin's* (1960), *I'm Sorry* (1960), *Dum Dum* (1961) and *All Alone Am I* (1962). In 1969 she returned to the country market with *Johnny One Time* and has remained there ever since, although many of her recordings have a much broader musical base than normal Nashville country fare. One of her most successful recent singles was *Broken Trust* (1980) which also featured the Oak Ridge Boys.

The Everly Brothers proved the exception to the rule that a rockabilly act, after pop-chart success, would return to country roots. Their greatest success was as a pop act, although their initial recordings also fared well in the country charts. The brothers, Don (born Brownie, Kentucky, 1 February 1937) and Phil (born 19 January 1939), were born into purest country traditions – their parents were singers Ike and Margaret Everly. After making their preteen radio debut on KMA in Shenandoah, Iowa, they worked with their parents as a family act until they graduated from high school, then they quit and headed out to Nashville. There, in the Acuff-Rose offices, they met up with songwriters Felice and Boudleaux Bryant, a meeting that led to an artists/writers/publishing-house association that would last for several years and result in millions of singles and albums sales. It commenced, on Cadence Records, with the million-selling *Bye Bye Love* (1957) and continued with such as *Wake Up Little Susie* (1957), *All I Have To Do Is Dream* (1958) and *('Til) I Kissed You* (1959), scoring sixteen country-rock successes before switching to Warner Bros. in 1960. In 1973, after a lifetime of working together (and experiencing the feuds that such closeness would bring), the Everlys finally went their own way. It was only the determined efforts from Britain (where the duo's popularity has never faltered, and sales of reissues have hardly slipped) that brought them back together again – for two memorable evening concerts at London's prestigious Albert Hall in late 1983.

The effect of the rockabilly boom was to change the face of popular music, as well as make its effect felt within country circles. Some country singers were the cause of the changes, others reaped its reward before making their way back to their country base. Others even attempted to fit into the movement when their record sales started to drop. Some were successful, like 'Tennessee' Ernie Ford who cut the Merle Travis mining song *Sixteen Tons* (1955) with a pseudo-rock accompaniment and got himself one of the fastest-selling singles in American music history. Others didn't fare quite as well, their more mature voices hardly appealing to the younger audiences. Even the king of western swing, Bob Wills, made a bid, with the result that some of his mid-1950s Decca cuts sounded just a little adventurous even for him.

Fearing that country could be completely obliterated by the rock avalanche, the industry started to fight back, adopting the premise that if country couldn't win on its own account then it would have to win by changing its sounds and structure. When Sonny James became the first country singer to top the pop charts with *Young Love* (1957), a song that had direct appeal to the youth market and possessed little hint of normal country instrumentation, the industry knew that it was on the right track. Within six months Ferlin Husky (*Gone*), Marty Robbins (*A White Sport Coat*) and Marvin Rainwater (*Gonna Find Me A Bluebird*) had also scored high pop-chart placings. The beliefs were confirmed. The Nashville Sound was on its way.

The Nashville Sound

By the beginning of the 1960s the rockabilly boom was all but over and the Nashville Sound was fast on its way to establishing Nashville as the country-music capital of the world. More records by country artists were surfacing in the pop charts, like Johnny Horton's *Battle Of New Orleans* (1959) and Jim Reeves' chart topping *He'll Have To Go* (1960), and the Everly Brothers, Brenda Lee, Elvis Presley and Roy Orbison were among the singers who proved that the city could produce pop records as good as anywhere else. Then, in January 1962, another landmark was achieved as Ray Charles released his million-selling *Modern Sounds Of Country And Western Music* album and, during the following months, scored high pop single-chart placings with distinctive interpretations of the country songs *I Can't Stop Loving You, You Are My Sunshine, Your Cheating Heart* and *Take These Chains From My Heart* showing that country was for all singers and all audiences.

The creation of the Nashville Sound saw the birth of a new era in country, which not only established the importance of Nashville as a major recording center (quickly to rival New York and Los Angeles) but also opened up the pathway to a highly commercial sound that would lead to the multimillion dollar crossover market a decade later.

The Nashville Sound itself is a little hard to define, it being a looseness in presentation and a move away from hard-core country instrumentation and a step nearer pop. Fiddles, representing the more solid sound of country, were out, though violins, the 'softer' pop equivalent, were acceptable (and used more and more as the years passed). The steel guitar initially took a back seat, and was reintroduced by the country-rock bands of the late 1960s, who used the instrument prominently in their lineups. The Sound was created out of the Nashville studios and blossomed thanks to the efforts of producers, musicians and other key persons, who provided innovative touches and a casual, informal approach to their work.

Chet Atkins was a prime mover in its development although, against popular myth, he won't admit to being the movement's founder. 'I didn't create the Nashville Sound,' he explains, 'it was a bunch of musicians and other a&r people who had a lot to do with it, but I guess it was because I had gotten a name as a guitar player that people tend to credit me for it. The intention of the sound was clear enough though – it was to sell more records.'

A Tennessean (born Luttrell, 20 June 1924), Atkins started his career as a guitarist, playing on various Southern radio stations and working with groups such as the Carter Family (Mother May-

belle and daughters June, Helen and Anita) and Shorty Thompson and his Rangers – 'I moved around a lot, I got fired from every job I ever had.' Eventually he came to the attention of RCA's Steve Shoals who was in charge of country-music recordings and operated out of New York. Curiously, Atkins' first recordings mainly featured him as a vocalist, but it was the instrumentals that received the airplays. In 1949 he gained even greater attention with cuts such as *Canned Heat* and *Country Gentleman* and, the following year, made the move to Nashville. He continues the story:

> Mr. Sholes was making trips from New York every two or three months to handle productions and I started hiring the musicians and arranging the dates. Eventually I would teach the artists the songs but, when he discovered Elvis Presley and gotten more important to the label, he would call me up and say that he was sending some songs down and want me to record the artists, like Johnny and Jack, or Jim Reeves, or Hank Snow. So, by and by, he didn't come down to Nashville at all and I ended up making all

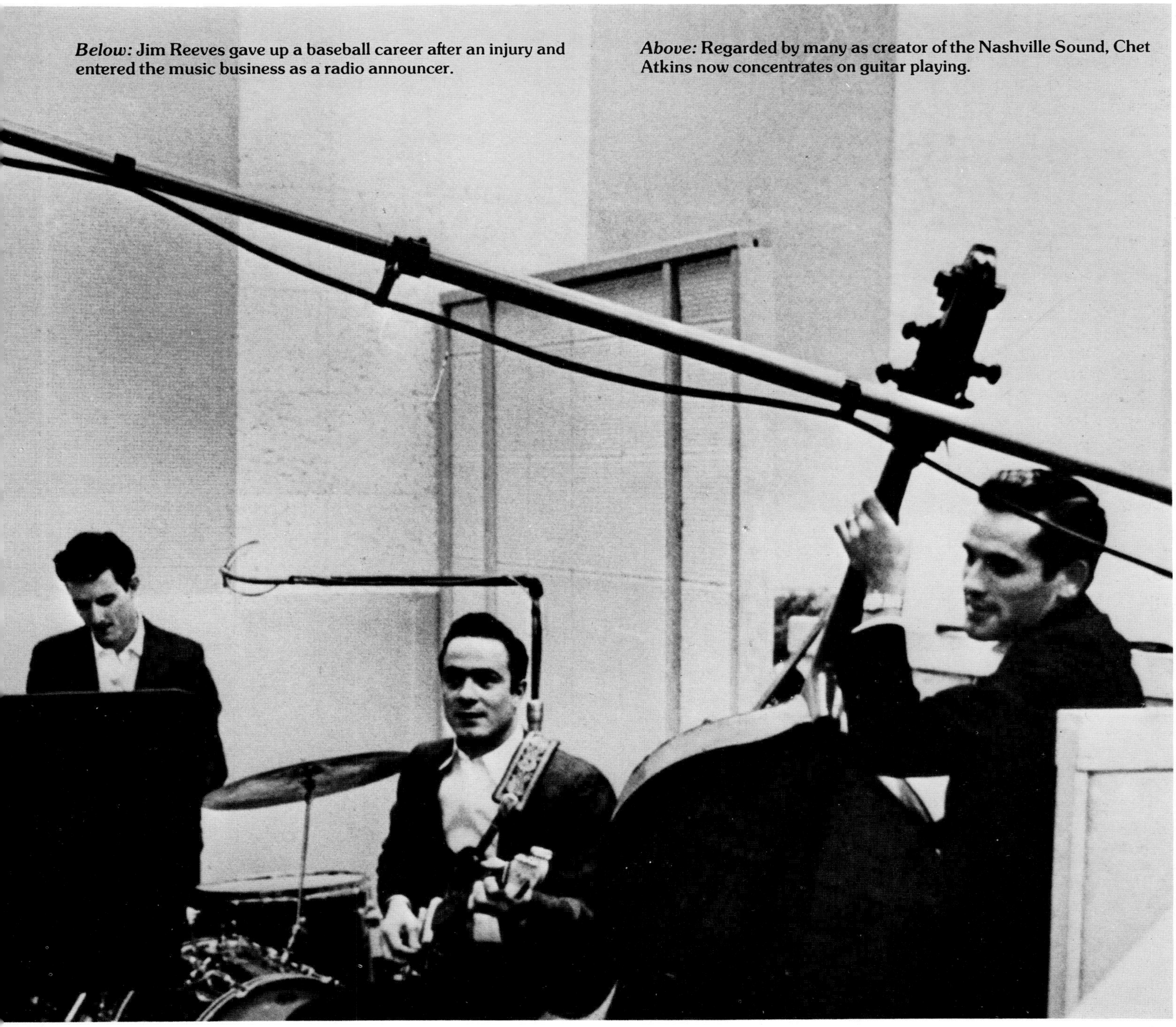

Below: **Jim Reeves gave up a baseball career after an injury and entered the music business as a radio announcer.**

Above: **Regarded by many as creator of the Nashville Sound, Chet Atkins now concentrates on guitar playing.**

Above: Steve Sholes is responsible for country music at RCA.
Left: Owen Bradley started out as a pianist and now records much of the top country talent for Decca and for his own studio.
Below: The Nashville skyline, the home of country music.

the records. He was paying me $75 a week as a retainer and I, of course, played on some of the records and picked up $50 or $60 for that. But the money wasn't important . . . I loved it and I was getting to do what I wanted to do.

Atkins also recalls that his initial, biggest problem in handling the production himself was honest-to-goodness fear, though this was swiftly overcome when Don Gibson was booked for one of his earliest sessions. The songs cut included *Oh Lonesome Me* and *I Can't Stop Loving You.* The results were one-million sales, a breakthrough into both the country and pop charts and considerable success overseas when released in early 1958. The story behind that session, as Atkins recalls, also gives an insight into how the Nashville Sound came into existence.

I had signed up Don Gibson in 1956 or '57. He had been on several labels, including RCA before as well as MGM and Columbia and I had worked with him as a sessionman, but nothing had happened with his records. I had seen something in him though, he had started to write and he was different. Steve Sholes was hesitant because of the earlier lack of success, and we had to record him real country at first because Wesley Rose, whom Don had a publishing deal with at Acuff-Rose, wanted it that way and he was a real aggressive guy. So we recorded him with fiddles and steel guitar – and nothing happened again. So I said, 'okay we'll do it my way now' and on that session we used a real heavy drum beat and I played an electric guitar solo through an echo device which was very infectious, I guess. The record turned out a real big hit and was one of the recordings that helped launch the Nashville Sound. What we had on it were new sounds and it just proved that, when people buy records, they want surprises. They want new sounds and I guess that was the foundation of the Nashville Sound.

***Above:* British-born Don Law was the chief country executive for Columbia Records, when they set up offices in Nashville in 1961.**

By the end of the 1960s Chet Atkins, then an RCA Vice President, had made full use of the Nashville Sound in developing one of country's strongest rosters of artists, bringing to the forefront of the scene the talents of Jim Reeves, Skeeter Davis, Don Gibson, George Hamilton IV, Bobby Bare, The Browns (and, later, Jim Ed Brown as a solo artist), Hank Locklin, Charley Pride and Jerry Reed among others.

The other major force in Nashville's modern-day development was Owen Bradley, Decca's chief country executive and founder of the most used studio in town. Another native of Tennessee (he was born in rural Westmoreland), Bradley started out as a pianist playing both country and pop before becoming leader of the WSM orchestra in 1947, a position he held for more than ten years. Around that time he became assistant country-music director at Decca under Paul Cohen (as well as making a number of records, one of them, *White Silver Sands*, under the guise of the Owen Bradley Quintet, making the pop charts in 1957) and, when Cohen moved on to Coral Records, he assumed full responsibility for the label's country product. In 1961 he was named 'Country & Western Man Of The Year' by Billboard magazine, while his Bradley Studio worked near to capacity. Averaging some 700 sessions a year, the studio recorded pop singers like Connie Francis and Guy Mitchell as well as his own productions on country talent that included Patsy Cline, Brenda Lee, Bill Monroe, Ernest Tubb and Kitty Wells. Later he became the guiding light behind the successful careers of such as Loretta Lynn, Conway Twitty and Jack Greene.

Columbia Records was the third major label to build up a substantial country roster, setting up offices in Nashville in late 1961

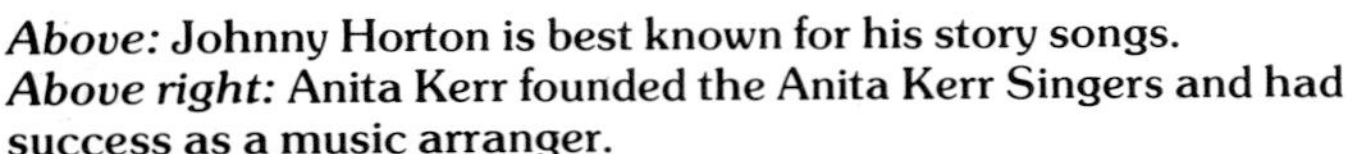

Above: Johnny Horton is best known for his story songs.
Above right: Anita Kerr founded the Anita Kerr Singers and had success as a music arranger.
Below: The Jordanaires, originally a gospel-music quartet, have been recording for 20 years.
Right, both: Chet Atkins was known as 'Mr. Guitar.'

under the auspices of its country head, British-born Don Law. (Prior to Law taking over responsibilities, the country duties were shared between him and another British expatriot, one-time 1920s field scout Art Satherley – an agreement that saw Satherley recording all country artists west of El Paso and Law taking care of the eastern section.) It was Don Law who persuaded Columbia to purchase Owen Bradley's 16th Avenue South 'Quonset' hut studio in 1962 – Bradley, by that time had his equally-famous 'Barn' studio in operation – as well as working with artists such as Johnny Cash, Marty Robbins, Lefty Frizzell and Lester Flatt and Earl Scruggs up until his retirement in the mid-1960s.

The Nashville Sound was built upon the skills of musicians and vocal groups but, during the late 1950s, there was a very limited choice of either. Harold Bradley was one of the first session players, having gained experience working as a member of Ernest Tubb's Texas Troubadours, while elder brother Owen frequently sat in as pianist – until his workload got cut down when Floyd Cramer arrived in town from the Louisiana Hayride. (Besides becoming one of Nashville's busiest musicians, Cramer also helped to spread the Nashville Sound message by scoring three massive county-pop hits during 1960-61, *Last Date, On The Rebound* and *San Antonio Rose.*) Atkins also, of course, played an immensely important role as a sessionman. Other musicians who worked in the Nashville recording studios around this time included: guitarists Grady Martin, Hank Garland, Ray Edenton and Jerry Reed; bass players Bob Moore and Junior Husky; drummers Buddy Harmon and D J Fontana, (he came to town with Presley); and steel guitarists Jerry Byrd, 'Little' Roy Wiggins and Pete Drake (of 'talking steel guitar' fame who chalked up a pop hit with *Forever* in 1964).

The Jordanaires – comprising Gordon Stoker (first tenor), Hoyt Hawkins (baritone), Neal Matthews (second tenor) and Ray Walker (bass) – also spent several years with Presley, working on both his recordings and movie soundtracks. Originally a gospel-music quartet, they were kept extremely busy during the initial days

Above: Don Gibson helped put the Nashville Sound on the map and scored more hits for himself, including *Sea of Heartbreak* and *Blue, Blue Day*.
Above right and right: Chet Atkins *(above)* encouraged Skeeter Davis back into the recording scene as a solo artist and his productions put her at the top of the charts.
Below right: Former recording partners Skeeter Davis and George Hamilton IV re-create a couple of hits at the International Festival of Country Music in London.
Below: George Hamilton IV earned his tag as 'International Ambassador of Country Music' through his many overseas tours. In 1971 he recorded one of his first television series for the BBC in London.

of the Nashville Sound and today, over twenty years later, remain an integral part of the recording scene.

The other important vocal group of the period was the Anita Kerr Singers. Its founding member – Memphis-born Anita Kerr (born 13 October 1927) – also contributed to the Sound as one of its most successful arrangers. Possessing a background as pianist and orchestrator, Kerr was first heard in Nashville heading an eight-piece choir on WSM's *Sunday Down South*, an assignment that led to recording sessions with Decca – Red Foley's *Our Lady Of Fatima* (1950) saw the debut of the Anita Kerr Singers – and spots on the Grand Ole Opry as an accordionist. But it was through working with Atkins that the group's smooth sounds were first heard to full effect, with their leader subsequently getting the opportunity to show off her arranging skills. Kerr's talents cannot be underestimated when noting that she contributed to some of the biggest country-pop hits of the period, including Jim Reeves' *He'll Have To Go* (1960), Floyd Cramer's *Last Date* (1960) (for which she wrote a ten-part string arrangement in ten minutes in the absence of the booked arranger, states Atkins), Skeeter Davis' *End Of The World* (1962), Bobby Bare's *Detroit City* and Reeves' *Welcome To My World* (1964). Atkins also recorded the Anita Kerr Singers in their own right as well as touring with them overseas. In the 1960s, looking for pastures new, Anita Kerr based herself in Hollywood, winning three Grammy Awards in 1965/66 and working with such as Henry Mancini and Rod McKuen.

The most successful artist to emerge on the strength of the Nashville Sound was undoubtedly Jim Reeves (born Panola County, Texas, 20 August 1923). Known as 'Gentleman Jim,' he possessed a smooth vocal styling that perfectly fitted the new emerging sounds. He initially pursued a baseball career and had signed a contract with the St Louis Cardinals when a leg injury cut short such ambitions. Instead he started radio announcing on KWKH, which gave him an opening to the Louisiana Hayride and the local Abbott Records. In 1953 he topped the Country Charts with *Mexican Joe*, a hard-core uptempo country song, and quickly followed through with another best seller, *Bimbo*, and attracted interest from both RCA and the Grand Ole Opry. In 1955 he scored his first major label success with the original composition *Yonder Comes A Sucker*. But Atkins saw other qualities in Reeves' voice and started projecting its easy-listening appeal with a series of ballads, first hitting the top of the charts with *Four Walls* (1957). Within two years the major breakthrough came with *He'll Have To Go*.

Tragically Reeves was never to realize his greatest glories, nor know the considerable contributions he made to country-pop music, dying in a plane crash on 31 July 1964, after negotiating a property deal in Arkansas. Within three years of that fateful day, the Reeves' name was linked with six number 1s – *I Guess I'm Crazy* (1964), *This Is It* (1965), *Is It Really Over* (1965), the million-selling *Distant Drums* (1966), *Blue Side Of Lonesome* (1966) and *I Won't Come In While He's There* (1967) – as well as many millions of sales overseas. In Britain he was one of the most consistent artists in the pop charts, with more than two-dozen hits while in South Africa, where he had made his only movie, *Kimberley Jim* (1963), the Reeves' name drew success second to none.

The artist's recordings have continued to be released over the years, thanks to the shrewd business maneuvers of his widow Mary and a considerable catalog of unissued items. Already-issued items also were given facelifts by adding fresh string arrangements and other instrumentation and, recently, the voice of Deborah Allen was added to provide duet interpretations on a trio of songs including *Take Me In Your Arms And Hold Me* (1980). Reeves was elected into the Country Music Hall of Fame in 1967, while his countless fans now annually make pilgrimages to the Jim Reeves Museum, opened in 1981 and situated on the site of a historic plantation ten miles north of Nashville.

Above: **Jim Reeves, 'Gentleman Jim,' was elected to the Country Music Hall of Fame posthumously.**
Left: **Patsy Cline brought country music to a mass audience.**

Reeves' female counterpart was Patsy Cline (born Winchester, Virginia, 8 September 1932), the possessor of an ice-cool yet powerful voice who, for an all too brief period, held both the country and the pop world in the palm of her hand. Sadly her life was too short and her output of recording material too small. Like Reeves, she perished in a plane crash on 5 March 1963, which also took the lives of stalwart performers Cowboy Copas and Hawkshaw Hawkins. She had the ultimate honor bestowed upon her, posthumously, with admission to the Country Music Hall of Fame in 1973.

She broke into the bigtime after winning top prize on Arthur Godfrey's Talent Scout show in 1957 by singing *Walkin' After Midnight*, a song that was to provide her with a Decca contract and her first chart success. By the beginning of the 1960s she was the biggest attraction on the Opry and the first serious threat to Kitty Wells' 'Queen Of Country' tag as she held on to the highest regions of the charts with *I Fall To Pieces* (1961), *Crazy* (1962) and *She's Got You* (1962), all easily fitting into the country-pop mold and hardly dating with the passing of the years. Like Reeves, she helped bring Nashville's music to a mass public – and a sound of country music rarely heard before. They never recorded together but it seemed a natural enough occurrence that some 20 years later, thanks to Owen Bradley and a masterful feat of studio technology, they were heard together on *Have You Ever Been Lonely* and *I Fall To Pieces*, both released during the period 1981/82.

Another victim of a particularly tragic era was Johnny Horton (born Tyler, Texas, 3 April 1929), 'the Singing Fisherman,' whose death occurred in an automobile accident just eighteen months after his biggest triumph with *Battle Of New Orleans* (1959). He was another singer to have gained recognition from Louisiana Hayride appearances (and, later, to have his own television series originating from his home town of Tyler). His chart appearances, on Columbia, were launched with *Honky Tonk Man* (1956). Although his recordings were much more deep rooted in country than the Nashville Sound, he did occasionally make use of strings – as heard on his Number 1 single *When It's Springtime In Alaska*

(1959) – though his greatest successes came with story songs like *New Orleans, Johnny Reb* (1959), *Sink The Bismarck* (1960) and the movie theme *North To Alaska* (1960).

If any one label was directly linked with the name 'Nashville Sound' then it has to be RCA, which even had the words blazed across the album jackets on occasion. It helped to build careers, though a number of them were really only successful during the Sound's most publicized days. Skeeter Davis (born Mary Frances Penick) had her first hit as a member of the Davis Sisters with *I Forgot More Than You'll Ever Know* (1953). When her friend Betty Jack Davis died in an auto accident, it was Atkins who persuaded her to recommence singing as a solo artist. Frequently having her voice double tracked (to overcome its shortcomings), she became one of Nashville's top stars with singles like *(I Can't Help It) I'm Falling Too* (1960), *My Last Date (With You)* (1961) and the million-selling *The End Of The World* (1962).

Florida's Hank Locklin kicked off his recording career on Four Star in the late 1940s, though RCA consolidated his chart position with country-pop hits that included *Geisha Girl* (1957), *Send Me The Pillow You Dream On* (1958) and *Please Help Me I'm Falling* (1960), a plea quickly answered by Skeeter Davis. The hits continued throughout the decade and he even recorded some items with the innovative, though relatively unsuccessful (in chart terms), Danny Davis & The Nashville Brass. The Browns, featuring Jim Ed and his sisters Maxine and Bonnie, had also gained popularity before RCA came along, having been regulars on the Louisiana Hayride and Ozark Jubilee and enjoying releases on the Abbott label. Jim Reeves brought the trio to Atkins and they quickly scored a million sales with *The Three Bells* (based on the French *Les Trois Cloches*) in 1959, following up with other biggies like *Scarlet Ribbons* (1959) and *The Old Lamplighter* (1960). Upon his sisters' retirement, Jim Ed Brown scored as a solo artist with *Pop A Top* (1967) and *Morning* (1970), though his biggest success came when he joined with singer/songwriter Helen Cornelius on a string of duet hits, commencing with a Number 1 *I Don't Want To Have To Marry You* (1976). Connie Smith's success, however, was born directly out of the Nashville Sound and achieved the label's biggest record of the year in 1964 with *Once A Day*, following her discovery by Bill Anderson. She subsequently notched up more than 30 chart entries, including *Ain't Had No Lovin'* (1966) and *Just One Time* (1971), but these days she mainly confines herself to gospel music and appearances on the Grand Ole Opry.

George Hamilton IV (born Winston-Salem, North Carolina, 19 July 1937) started off in fine style with the million-selling *A Rose And A Baby Ruth* (1956), which launched him as a pop star, and appeared on rock 'n' roll tour packages. It took the singer several years, a change of label and a relocation to Nashville before he gained recognition as a country artist. With Atkins producing, he broke through with such as *Before This Day Ends* (1960) and *Abilene* (1963). Hamilton was rather different from other country singers in that he looked further afield for his material (he was among the first to record songs by Gordon Lightfoot, Joni Mitchell and Buffy St Marie) as well as spending considerable time and effort in building up foreign popularity. He has worked extensively in Canada and Britain, and was the first country act to perform in Czechoslovakia and Russia, all of which earned him the title of 'The International Ambassador Of Country Music,' but his absences might well have contributed to the decline of his career in the States.

Bobby Bare (born Ironton, Ohio, 7 April 1935), who first claimed chart fame as Bill Parsons with *All American Boy* (1958),

Right and inset: **Bobby Bare kept in touch with the trends in music and has remained a top performer for nearly 25 years.**

BARE

Left: **Claude King provided the theme song, *The Commancheros*, for the John Wayne movie of the same title that was a hit in 1962. It sold a million.**
Above: **Country-pop singer Sonny James became the first country singer to reach the top of the pop charts. Twenty of his singles reached Number 1 between 1964-72.**

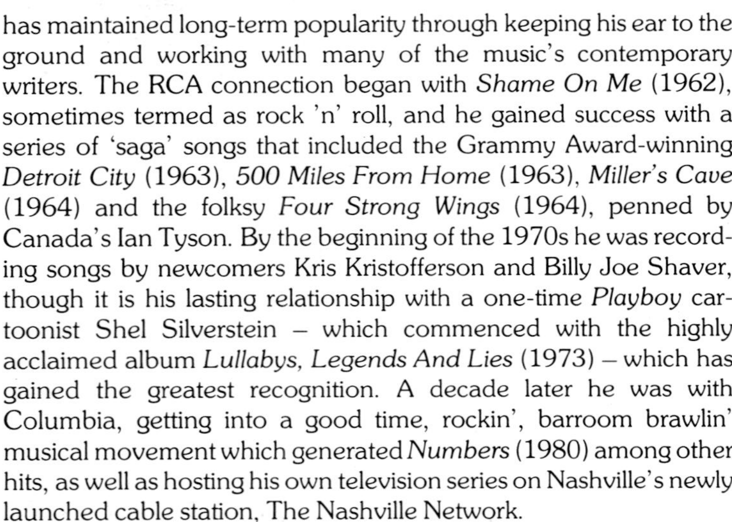

has maintained long-term popularity through keeping his ear to the ground and working with many of the music's contemporary writers. The RCA connection began with *Shame On Me* (1962), sometimes termed as rock 'n' roll, and he gained success with a series of 'saga' songs that included the Grammy Award-winning *Detroit City* (1963), *500 Miles From Home* (1963), *Miller's Cave* (1964) and the folksy *Four Strong Wings* (1964), penned by Canada's Ian Tyson. By the beginning of the 1970s he was recording songs by newcomers Kris Kristofferson and Billy Joe Shaver, though it is his lasting relationship with a one-time *Playboy* cartoonist Shel Silverstein – which commenced with the highly acclaimed album *Lullabys, Legends And Lies* (1973) – which has gained the greatest recognition. A decade later he was with Columbia, getting into a good time, rockin', barroom brawlin' musical movement which generated *Numbers* (1980) among other hits, as well as hosting his own television series on Nashville's newly launched cable station, The Nashville Network.

A direct descendant of Sam Houston and Robert E. Lee, David Houston (born Shreveport, Louisiana, 9 December 1938) is also assured of his place in the music history books as being one of the decade's biggest country hitmakers. He also made a pop breakthrough with *Almost Persuaded* (1966), a song that started life as a 'B' side but flipped over following enthusiastic deejay response. His first steps up the ladder came at the age of twelve, when he made a guest appearance on his home town's Louisiana Hayride. He later became a regular at the Hayride, and made his first recordings for Sun. But it was on the Epic label (which he, along with Tammy Wynette, developed as a major contender in the country market) that he reaped success, commencing with 300,000 sales with *Mountain Of Love* (1963) and continuing with twenty more chart entries before the end of the 1960s. Other major hits were *You Mean The World To Me* (1967), *Already It's Heaven* (1968) and *Baby Baby* (1969). The 1970s saw a fall in success status though Houston still continued to make the charts with regularity.

Arguably the most successful of artists to make full use of the country-pop sound was Sonny James (born Jimmie Loden in Hackleburg, Alabama, 1 May 1929) who claims the distinction of being the first country singer to top the pop charts (*Young Love* in 1957). During the period 1964-72, twenty out of 24 single releases made the top of the Billboard charts yet, strangely for a singer who succeeded with a hybrid sound, this singer's roots were more traditionally founded than most of his compatriots. He was raised with a musical family, made his stage debut at four and quickly became the master of the fiddle. After his military service (which included fifteen months in Korea), he linked up with Ken Nelson of Capitol Records, which resulted in his chart debut with *For Rent* (1956). His 1960s material comfortably fitted the country-pop mold, as was seen when Cliff Richard covered his *The Minute You're Gone* (1963) while *I'll Never Find Another You* and *A World Of Our Own* both originated from the Australian-founded, London-based Seekers group. Another of his chart toppers, *Running Bear* (1969), was first recorded during the rockabilly era by Johnny Preston. Nicknamed 'The Southern Gentleman,' James also appeared in a number of low-budget movies including *Hillbillies In A Haunted House* (1968), starring Basil Rathbone, and producing Marie Osmond's million-selling *Paper Roses* (1973).

The other country-pop successes of the period included Ned Miller, who originally recorded for the Fabor label and achieved international attention, albeit short-lived, with *From A Jack To A King* (1962) and *Do What You Do Do Well* (1965), and Shreveport's Claude King who, in 1962, collected a million sales with another saga song *The Commancheros*, the theme from the John Wayne movie of the same name. Jerry Wallace, from Alabama, regularly flitted between country and pop, first living up to his title 'Mr Smooth' with *Primrose Lane* (1959) and scoring around three-dozen successes during the following quarter of the century, including *If You Leave Me Tonight I'll Cry* (1972), the theme from Rod Serling's television series. Alabama's Bobby Goldsboro, who at one time worked for Roy Orbison as a guitarist, appealed to the emotions (and collected a million sales) with *Honey* (1968) – and continued to win over sentiments with *Watching Scotty Grow* (1971) and *A Butterfly For Bucky* (1976). There was also no holding back Eddy Arnold and Ray Price who, as noted earlier, made full use of strings and sophisticated arrangements to project their careers to even greater heights.

The early 1960s saw a new subject matter creeping into country – and fully exploited after Dave Dudley hit the top with *Six Days On The Road* (1963) – the truck-driving song, a genre that took the

place of the railroad men and cowboys of earlier times and represented one of the last areas of freedom as the truckers traveled the wide-open highways. There had been songs about truckers and their lifestyles before, like the Ted Daffan penned *Truck Driver Blues* and Lonnie Irving's *Pinball Machine* (1960), but Dudley's offering on Mercury put the movement into top gear and made his reputation. Although a fine ballad singer who has recorded other material he continued trucking with songs like *Truck Drivin' Son-Of-A-Gun* (1965) and *Trucker's Prayer* (1967). Other singers also found a ready niche with such material, including North Carolina-born Del Reeves (who had already scored a Number 1 in 1965 with *Girl On The Billboard*) with *Looking At The World Through A Windshield* (1968) and the West Coast's Red Simpson who virtually built a whole career on the strength of *Roll Truck Roll* (1966) and *I'm A Truck* (1971).

Then, in late 1975, the genre was expanded as CB radio crept into the picture and C W McCall – a pseudonym adopted by award-winning advertising executive William Fries – used its language to maximum effect in the multimillion-selling, international-hit *Convoy*, a song that later created an equally successful movie starring Kris Kristofferson. That same year Cledus Maggard took *The White Knight* to the top while, in 1976, veteran singer Red Sovine (who had already recorded the ultimate trucking ghost story in *Phantom 309*) achieved the biggest hit of his career with the heart-rending tale of a crippled boy, CB radio and truckers in *Teddy Bear*, a million seller that found favor with all sections of the record-buying public. There was even a gay trucking song, Rod Hart's *C.B. Savage* (1976), though this didn't find favor with all deejays.

Equally as important as the artists, musicians and producers were the songwriters who provided the raw material for the Nashville Sound success. Traditionally, many country singers penned their own songs but, during the late 1940s and 1950s, this started changing with the emergence of professional writers coming up with material specifically for the country market. Fred Rose was one of the first, and his *Blue Eyes Crying In The Rain* ranks as a standard, and was followed by such as Vaughan Horton, the composer of *Teardrops In My Heart* and *Mockingbird Hill* among others, and Cy Coben, who wrote many hits for such as Eddy

Above and above left: **In the 1960s Dave Dudley, in concert and leaning against the truck, found fame and fortune with a new brand of truck-driving ballads such as *Truck Drivin' Son-Of-a-Gun.***
Below: **William Fries, better known as C W McCall, was the advertising executive who made a hit out of the song *Convoy*.**

Arnold and Hank Snow. Undoubtedly the most successful writers of the late 1950s were the husband and wife team of Felice and Boudleaux Bryant who penned many of the Everly Brothers hits, as well as other best sellers like Bob Luman's *Let's Think About Living (1960), Ray Price's She Wears My Ring* (1968) and the much recorded classic *Rocky Top*. Kentucky's Harlan Howard was to become the most successful honky-tonk styled writer of the period, coming up with hits like *Pick Me Up On Your Way Down, I Fall To Pieces, Busted* and *Heartaches By The Number* and earning for himself (in 1961) numerous awards and well over £100,000 in royalties. John D. Loudermilk – who established his reputation, as well as that of George Hamilton IV, with *A Rose And A Baby Ruth* (1956) – created such hits as *Tobacco Road, Abilene* and *Break My Mind* as well as establishing a minor recording career for himself with *Language Of Love* (1961).

Then there were the successful entertainers who first gained the industry's attention as songwriters, in particular Bill Anderson and Mel Tillis. Anderson (born Columbia, South Carolina, 1 November 1937), nicknamed 'Whispering Bill' because of his soft vocal styling, started out from the University of Georgia as a journalist and moved over to disc jockey work before Ray Price rose to the top of the charts with Anderson's *City Lights* (1958). Other artists like Faron Young, Jim Reeves and Porter Wagoner quickly started cutting Anderson songs, which led to the writer securing his own recording contract with Decca – and a chart debut with *That's What It's Like To Be Lonesome* (1959). His first Number 1 came with the narration *Mama Sang A Song* (1962) and, the following year, he advanced his popularity by landing *Still* high in the pop charts. All in all he totaled more than 40 albums and 50 hits, including more Number 1s with *I Get The Fever* (1966), *For Loving You* (1967, a duet with his road-show singer Jan Howard), *World Of Make Believe* (1973) and *Sometimes* (1976, another duet, this time with later road-show singer Mary Lou Turner) as well as attempting to bring disco into country with *I Can't Wait Any Longer* (1978). He still continues to record but, during recent years, has made inroads into television as an actor and quiz- and chat-show host.

Above: Over the course of his 25-year career, Bill Anderson successfully combined songwriting with recording and television.
Right: **Mel Tillis, the creator of *Ruby, Don't Take Your Love to Town*, is shown winning fans during his first British appearance at the Wembley Festival in 1983. He won the CMA Entertainer of the Year Award in 1976. Recently he has moved into movies.**
Below: **A stalwart performer for five decades, Red Sovine had amazing pop chart success in his late fifties when he scored with the million-selling CB song *Teddy Bear*.**

Mel Tillis (born Tampa, Florida, 8 August 1932), who started to write while serving in the Air Force, arrived in Nashville in 1957 and scored some minor chart action on a series of labels but stirred up a lot of response (and substantial royalties) as the writer of songs like *Detroit City, Honky Tonk Song* and *Ruby, Don't Take Your Love To Town*. By the beginning of the 1970s his records were attracting more attention, with *Heart Over Mind* (1970) on Kapp, gaining a Top 3 placing and, with a new deal with MGM, hit the top with a revival of *I Ain't Never* (1972), originally co-penned with Webb Pierce. With more biggies under his belt, and leading an impressive road band that included a three-fiddle lineup, he won the CMA Entertainer Of The Year award in 1976. This award also marked his talents as a comedian, which generally centered around a stutter that affected his speech but never his songs. Although he still continues to score the hits, including the Number 1s *I Believe In You* (1978) and *Coca Cola Cowboy* (1979), Tillis has been recently diversifying his activities and appearing in movies like *W. W. & The Dixie Dancekings* (1975) and *Smokey And The Bandit II* (1980).

Undoubtedly the most successful singer/songwriter of the 1960s was Roger Miller (born Fort Worth, Texas, 2 January 1936), the madcap genius whose sardonic humor and fresh, unpredictable lyrics won him millions of record sales, an unprecedented eleven Grammy Awards in two years and opened the doors to a new generation of country songwriters. Hank Williams was his biggest influence and, after his discharge from the Army, he headed for Nashville where he stayed his first night in the Andrew Jackson Hotel and the next morning applied for (and got) a job as bellhop.

Ray Price was the first to record a Miller song, *Invitation To The Blues* (1958), and used him in his band, as did Faron Young. Other artists to ride to success with a Miller song included Jim Reeves (*Billy Bayou*) and Ernest Tubb (*Half A Mind*). As a recording artist he achieved a Top 10 hit with *When Two Worlds Collide* on RCA in 1961, but three years later (and a change to Smash, a division of Mercury Records) he cast aside all songwriting logic and staggered both country and pop circles with a string of hits that would earn him the highest awards in the industry. The titles underline his nonsensical appraoch – *Dang Me, Chug-A-Lug, Do-Wacka-Do, England Swings* and *You Can't Roller Skate In A Buffalo Herd* – while his straighter *King Of The Road* provided the name for the string of motels that he was to open up with part of the rewards reaped by such eccentricities. Sadly the period 1964/65 saw his real glory days and, although he continued to record and made soundtracks for the movies *Waterhole 3* (1967) and Walt Disney's *Robin Hood* (1973), he never came near to repeating such success, nor was ever likely to.

One of the writers to benefit from Miller presenting a new face to country was Tom T Hall (born Olive Hill, Kentucky, 25 May 1936), known to some as the 'Nashville Story Teller' and to others as the 'Mark Twain of Country Music,' though both titles clearly reflect Hall's skills in developing musical tales out of, sometimes, the most minimal foundations. The son of a preacher, Hall first gained musical experience by forming a bluegrass band (The Kentucky Travellers), before working on AFN radio in Germany during his Army stint, an occupation he later continued with while sending songs around Nashville. His first success came when Jimmy Newman recorded *D.J. For A Day* (1963), and this was followed by Dave Dudley's cut of *Mad* (1964). His status shot to top grade in 1968 with the multimillion-selling *Harper Valley PTA,* a song that made a star out of former Nashville secretary Jeannie C Riley (who then continued to turn out hit records, though none as big) and put Shelby Singleton's fledgling Plantation label on the map. By this

Above: **Felice and Boudleaux Bryant, early country music pair.**
Left: Detroit City **was one of Mel Tillis' many hits as a songwriter before he started achieving success as a star in his own right.**

Left: Nobody equalled Roger Miller's success as an innovative songwriter and singer during the 1960s.

Above: Connie Smith is another of the successes from the 1960s. Her singing career these days encompasses gospel music.

time Hall was also recording and achieved a Top 10 breakthrough with *Ballad Of Forty Dollars* (1968), and made it to Number 1 with *A Week In A County Jail* (1969). He scored a couple of dozen chart hits including the beautifully plaintive *Old Dogs, Children And Watermelon Wine* (1972) and a pop crossover with *I Love* (1974) and, after a relatively quiet relationship with RCA, returned to his former label, Mercury, with *Everything From Jesus To Jack Daniels* (1983).

A stabilizing force in the growth of country was the creation of the Country Music Association, a trade organization born in 1958 when the music was at its lowest ebb and developed through the efforts of its founders, Wesley Rose, Connie B Gay and Dee Kilpatrick and the office 'girl Friday,' Jo Walker (today, Jo Walker-Meador, and the Association's executive director). It was supported by an initial membership of 223 persons and its aim was to 'improve, market and publicize' country music, with its first target being the radio stations. Its success can be realized by looking at the figures: in 1961 there were only 81 full-time country stations, 21 years later the total stood at 2114 with an additional 941 programing the music on a part-time basis. Today the membership stands at more than 7000.

The CMA, which upholds its boast as 'America's most active trade organization,' played a major role, alongside the Nashville

Left: **Loretta Lynn came into the spotlight in the 1960s with the help of her promoter-husband. From country superstar she's now an internationally known personality.**
Above: **It made no difference to fans whether Conway Twitty sang rock or country; he was still a number-one performer.**
Below: **Tom T Hall was a successful singer of musical tales.**

Left: Loretta Lynn, the coal miner's daughter, whose success spawned a best-selling autobiograpy and top-grossing movie, and sold over 50 hit singles for herself.

Above: Loretta Lynn and Conway Twitty, business partners and occasional duet-recording artists, join forces in song during an early 1970s London visit.

Below: **The Country Music Hall of Fame presents the past, present and future of country music through sight and sound. Displays include Minnie Pearl's hat and Elvis Presley's cadillac.**

Sound, in broadening the scope of the music and getting it heard by new audiences. One of its major achievements was securing network-television coverage of its annual Awards in 1968 (a year after they were established), thanks to the efforts of Kraft Foods, still the show's major sponsor, and Walter Thompson: Among its other successes was the establishment of the Country Music Hall of Fame in 1961, the founding of the Country Music Foundation in 1964, and the opening of the Country Music Hall of Fame and Museum in 1967, a haven for country fans ever since. It participates every October in the WSM Birthday celebrations (once known as the 'Disc Jockey Convention') and, in June 1972, launched Fan Fair, an annual event which now sees more than 15,000 country music enthusiasts making the trek to Nashville to indulge themselves in a week-long round of stage shows, celebrity events, booth attractions and – most important – an opportunity to meet with the stars.

As the CMA grew in strength during the 1960s, new stars developed on country's home front. Three of them – Loretta Lynn, Tammy Wynette and Charley Pride – remain as big today as they ever were.

Loretta Lynn's success is a rags to riches tale, a story known to millions through her best-selling autobiography (and, later, top-grossing movie), *Coal Miner's Daughter*. Born Loretta Webb (Butcher's Hollow, Kentucky, 14 April 1935), the second of eight children to a Van Lears' coalminer, she married Oliver 'Mooney' Lynn at the age of thirteen and was encouraged into a country-music career by her husband. He then virtually single-handedly promoted her first single, *Honky Tonk Girl* (1960) on the small Zero label, by driving his wife around radio stations. It resulted in a Top 20 entry in the Billboard charts, a tie-up with Grand Ole Opry performers, The Wilburn Brothers, an introduction to producer Owen Bradley, who viewed her as a 'female Hank Williams,' and a recording deal with Decca. (She also received a great deal of encouragement from Patsy Cline, with whom she became friendly on the Opry and, in 1977, cut the tribute album *I Remember Patsy*.) By 1970 she had charted two-dozen hits, including the Number 1s *Don't Come Home A-Drinkin'* (1966), *Fist City* (1968) and *Woman Of The World (Leave My World Alone)* (1969) and was firmly established as the new 'Queen of Country.' She began the new decade with *Coal Miner's Daughter*, a song that said it all.

The past ten years – which has seen an unstoppable flow of hit records, including the controversial *The Pill* (1975) – has also seen Lynn emerge from country superstar to international personality, from CMA multiaward winner to being named as one of America's 100 Most Important Women and earning a place in Who's Who. She's also built up a substantial business empire, gone into partnership with Conway Twitty in the creation of the United Talent agency (as successful as the occasional duets on record) and, with hubby 'Mooney,' owns an entire Tennessean township – Hurricane Mills – which houses their colonial mansion and 1450 adjoining acres of ranch land. Strangely, the only thing that Loretta Lynn hasn't managed to do, to date, is get a single in the pop charts. Perhaps she's just a little too country for that!

Conway Twitty has also done pretty well in his own right, moving from a highly successful rock 'n' roll career and being just as triumphant with country, finding that his hard, driving vocals perfectly fitted the music's contemporary material. During his sixteen-year association with Decca/MCA, he scored around 60 hits, and more than half of them went right to the top. The pattern was set with *Next In Line* (1968), *To See My Angel Cry* (1969) and *15*

Years Ago (1970). *Hello Darlin'* (1970) touched around the million mark, as did *You've Never Been This Far Before* (1973), a song that – according to some sections of the industry and media – 'set new standards in dirty lyrics.' Unperturbed, the singer followed a few months later with the equally risque *(Lying Here With) Linda On My Mind* (1975). When he moved to Elektra, the hits went with him, one of his first successes being a country version of the Pointer Sisters' *Slow Hand* (1982). Away from the music, one of the singer's recent ventures has been the opening of his long-planned Twitty City, a theme park in Hendersonville that's 100 percent dedicated to his fans.

Loretta Lynn's biggest competition during the 1960s was Tammy Wynette (born Tupelo, Mississippi, 5 May 1942) who, in 1968, achieved the biggest selling single ever by a female country artist, *Stand By Your Man*. Although she had always wanted to be a singer, success didn't come easily and following an early marriage, the birth of three children and divorce, she held down a number of different jobs (including hairdressing) in order to meet medical bills. Eventually she started getting the right breaks and, with a few guest appearances on Porter Wagoner's television show to her credit, secured a deal with Epic Records. Once united with producer Billy Sherrill, with whom she joined forces on songwriting assignments, she soon hit the charts with *I Don't Want To Play House* (1967). She quickly established a recipe for success with heartbreaking themes, put over with utmost conviction by means of her plaintive 'sob in the voice' styling (earning her the description of 'country music's Edith Piaf'). Among her other memorable hits were *D-I-V-O-R-C-E* (1968), *Singing My Song* (1969), *Bedtime Story* (1972), *Kids Say The Darndest Things* (1973) and *'Til I Can Make It On My Own* (1976), as well as a number of top-rating duets with

Above and below: **Tammy Wynette with Billy Sherrill *(below)* and George Jones *(above)*. She has been called the 'Edith Piaf of Country Music' for her 'sob-in-the-voice' sound and the plaintive manner in which she handles her material.**

Top and above: Tammy Wynette, 'The First Lady of Country Music,' in concert in 1983.
Right: Tammy Wynette and George Jones, her one-time husband, at the Country Music Festival in 1981.

her one-time husband, George Jones. Her total record sales now well exceed the eighteen-million mark and, like Loretta Lynn, she is the recipient of many CMA Awards. She has also come up with a best-selling autobiography, *Stand By Your Man*, which reveals details of her stormy marriage with George Jones and an affair with Burt Reynolds.

The biggest breakthrough of the decade (or, for that matter, any other time in country history) was Charley Pride, the first black singer to establish himself as a superstar in the white man's music, although it caused the record label (RCA) some concern at the time of the singer's launch. Chet Atkins recalls:

> I worried about it a lot because I didn't know a heck of a lot about the people in Mississippi and Alabama, and was afraid that some of the record stations might block our records if we sent out Charley's single without some sort of explanation, and they'd later discover he was black and they had been tricked. But, in the end we let it go on its own merits and, if it were a hit, then we didn't owe anybody any apologies.

Born in Sledge, Mississippi (18 March 1938), Pride was one of eleven children. His early memories center around picking cotton and listening to the Grand Ole Opry. He had set career ambitions toward baseball (and had tried out for both the California Angels and the New York Mets) while also singing in local shows. It was at one of these performances that he was spotted by Red Sovine and Red Foley, who suggested that he try his luck in Nashville. Later Atkins came into the picture and the singer's career was launched

Above and right: **The 1960s saw an increase in female country singers. Loretta Lynn is shown above singing with her ex-husband George Jones and with members of her road show at London's International Festival of Country Music.**

with *The Snakes Crawl At Night*, released in January 1966. A few months later he made his chart debut with *Just Between You And Me* and, by the end of the decade, the Number 1s were stacking up and included *All I Have To Offer You (Is Me)* (1969), *(I'm So) Afraid Of Losing You Again* (1969) and *Is Anybody Goin' To San Antone* (1970). In 1971, he made the pop breakthrough with *Kiss An Angel Good Mornin'*, a million seller.

Today his credit stands at more than 50 hit singles, more than half of them chart toppers, including a couple of Hank Williams' revivals in 1980, *Honky Tonk Blues* and *You Win Again*. He's one of mainstream country's millionaire entertainers, a former CMA Entertainer of the Year (1971), the holder of a dozen gold discs and the owner of a successful management/agency company (Chadron) in Dallas. He gave a helping hand to such as Ronnie Milsap, Gary Stewart and Dave & Sugar when they were starting their careers. But, most of all, he's earned his place in the history books as the man who integrated country music. Charley Pride, however, views it more simply, 'I call it "skin hang-ups." I thought that I would just eliminate the "skin hang-ups" as a child and go about my business of being an individual. I'm an American singing American music – not a black man singing a white man's music.'

If the selection of star names for the 1960s were limited to one, then the name of Johnny Cash would rank highest. He remains one of the music's most durable, and beloved, entertainers. Yet his

Left and above: Charley Pride, the singer who integrated country music, though the launch of his career caused producer Chet Atkins some concern.

Above and right: **Johnny Cash and his wife, June Carter Cash, join David Frost (*left*) as guests on his television show.**

success hardly rolled with the Nashville Sound flow, he was his own master and he created his own sound, produced a number of highly acclaimed concept albums, scored around three-dozen hits in the ten-year period and, at the decade's end (1969) swept the CMA Awards by winning out in six categories including Entertainer, Album and Single as well as being presented with an Outstanding Services accolade.

Johnny Cash (born Kingsland, Arkansas, 26 February 1932) fits the genuine country mold. He was born into a rural environment (one of seven children in a poverty-ridden, cotton-picking family) and developed his craft of writing and singing to emerge as a twentieth-century troubadour. His music interest arose while serving with the Air Force in Germany and, after his discharge, he headed for Memphis where he was turned down initially by Sam Phillips. He continued working as an electrical-appliance salesman and joined forces with musicians Luther Perkins and Marshall Grant (later known as The Tennessee Two) and created a sound that impressed Phillips enough for him to sign the singer to a Sun Records deal, leading on to the initial record successes detailed above. By the end of the 1950s he had joined the Grand Ole Opry, made his motion-picture debut in the low-budgeted *Door To Door Maniac* (1958) and had scored his first Number 1 on his new label, Columbia, with *Don't Take Your Guns To Town* (1959).

The 1960s provided a real insight into the artist's considerable talents for, besides continuing his run of country and pop hits – which included *Ring Of Fire* (1963) and *Understand Your Man* (1964) – he started recording concept albums, a presentation virtually unknown in country circles. These covered subjects close to his heart and center around the folklore of the Old West, including *Ride This Train* (1960), dealing with railroads, trains and hobos; *Bitter Tears* (1964), detailing the plight of the Indians, a cause that continued to gain his full support; and the self-explanatory *Ballads Of The True West* (1965). By the end of the decade he had recorded his acclaimed, million-selling *Folsom* (1968) and *San Quentin* (1969) live-concert prison albums, gaining further support for his campaign for prison reform; had sat in on Bob Dylan's

Left and above: Johnny Cash has remained a music leader for close to 30 years. He duets with his wife, June Carter *(inset right)*. *Inset left:* The Carter Family on stage.

Above: Johnny Cash made his first movie in 1958.
Right and next page: Johnny Cash, 'The Man in Black,' has remained a country superstar for well over a quarter of a century. His roadshows include his wife and other members of the family.

Nashville Skyline (1969) sessions, and Dylan quickly repaid the compliment by appearing on Cash's network television series; continued to hit the chart's highspot with *Folsom Prison Blues* (1968), *Daddy Sang Bass* (1968, penned by Carl Perkins), *A Boy Named Sue* (1969, a Shel Silverstein novelty), *Sunday Morning Coming Down* (1970, gaining the first major award for then-struggling writer Kris Kristofferson) and *Flesh And Blood* (1970). In addition to the already-mentioned CMA Awards, which put the icing on the cake, he had also collected three Grammy Awards, including one for dueting with his wife June Carter on *Jackson* (1967). But, along with the good times, the singer pursued a lifestyle that saw him pill popping, boozing, missing dates and having minor run-ins with the law, making many believe that he could be heading for the same fate as Hank Williams. At his lowest ebb, Carl Perkins and June Carter remained his constant companions and helped him fight the battle for survival.

His activities were as diverse in the 1970s, with the decade commencing with two country-pop hits, *What Is Truth* and *If I Were A Carpenter* (another duet with wife June), and Hollywood beckoning for a starring role alongside Kirk Douglas in *A Gunfight*. There were a couple of special projects – he celebrated America's bicentennial four years before anyone else with the concept album *America: A 200 Year Salute In Story And Song* (1972), and mounted his own movie on the life of Christ by filming *The Gospel Road* in the Holy Land. In 1976 he scored another gigantic international hit with *One Piece At A Time*, and was back at the top of the country charts with *(Ghost) Riders In The Sky* (1979). Truly, Johnny Cash is a living legend, as well as being one of the music's elder statesmen. It goes without saying that his induction into the Country Music Hall of Fame in 1980 was ecstatically received by fans throughout the world.

Johnny Cash also headed one of the biggest roadshows in the business for several years, taking in his band The Tennessee Three (plus additional musicians, on occasion), June Carter, her mother Maybelle and sisters Anita and Helen (and, sometimes, additional kinfolk) and long-time friend Carl Perkins. For several years he was joined by the Statler Brothers, the quartet that set the pace for today's vocal groups. Originally a gospel-music quartet comprising brothers Don and Harold Reid, Phil Balsley and Lew DeWitt, all from Virginia, the Statlers burst upon the scene in 1965 with the million-selling country-pop hit *Flowers On The Wall*, penned by DeWitt. Their lasting success, however, began when they moved from Columbia to Mercury and recorded *Bed Of Rose's* (1970). The single set the pattern for good-sounding songs with attractive harmonies, frequently dipping into nostalgic themes that centered around the 1950s, Hollywood cowboys and personal memories – their greatest asset was that the majority of the songs stem from their own creative skills. Among their 40 or more hits are *Do You Remember These* (1972), *Whatever Happened To Randolph Scott* (1974), *Do You Know You Are My Sunshine* (1978) and *How To Be A Country Star* (1979), while building on their success by creating alter egos in the comic characters Lester 'Roadhog' Moran and the Cadillac Cowboys. Their popularity can be seen through the numerous awards they received, as well as walking away with the CMA Vocal Group trophy eight times during the period 1972-80. The only change in the Statlers' lineup occured in 1982 when Lew DeWitt retired through ill health (though he remains active in their business operations in Staunton, Virginia), his place being taken by Jimmy Fortune.

There were other successful newcomers during the 1960s, like Waylon Jennings and Willie Nelson, Dolly Parton and Barbara Mandrell, and no lesser person than the legend's son, Hank Williams Jr., but their initial success was nothing compared with what was to follow. Another age was coming to country music as Nashville Sound took a back seat to crossover, a movement that made even Chet Atkins ponder his responsibilities for taking country music 'too far uptown' in the first instance.

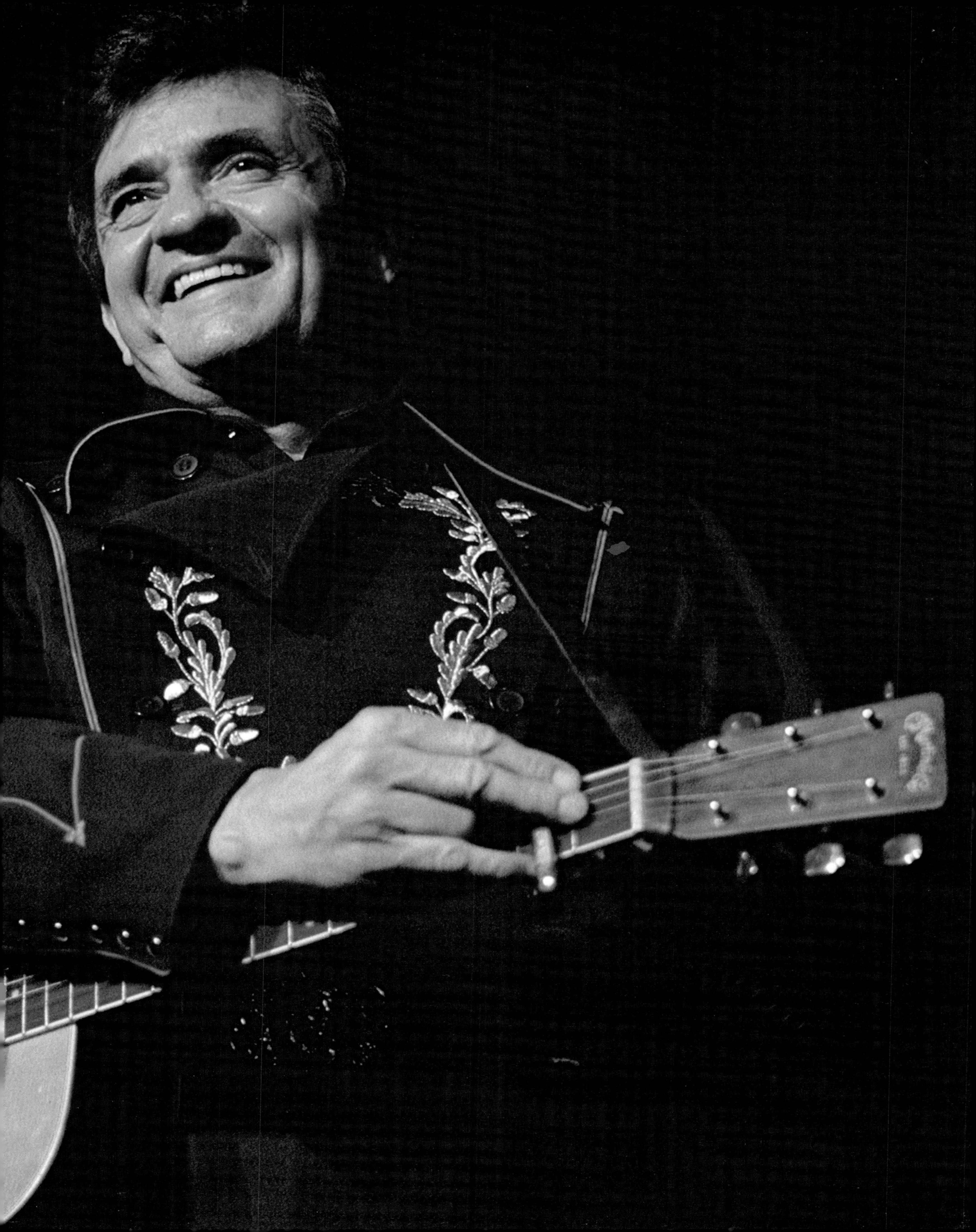

Country and Rock Out West

The Nashville Sound didn't get by without competition. There was a healthy scene flourishing out west in California, created out of the western swing and singing cowboy movements and supported by, above all, the migrant citizens. Such an audience was extensive, as revealed by a postwar survey which noted that 84 percent of the population of Southern California originally came from the southeastern and midwestern States.

Los Angeles had established a new industry and was further strengthened by the founding of Capitol Records in 1942. Lee Gillette was responsible for the label's country division and quickly signed Tex Ritter, Tex Williams, guitarist/singer/songwriter Merle Travis and 'Tennessee' Ernie Ford, the last named having relocated himself on the West Coast after Air Corps service. All were to become big sellers for the fledgling label.

'Tennessee' Ernie Ford (born Bristol, Tennessee, 19 February 1919), who had worked as a radio announcer prior to joining Cliffie Stone's Hometown Jamboree show, first started gaining the attention of country fans with *Smokey Mountain Boogie* (1949) and *Mule Train* (1949), as well as providing a foretaste of rockabilly with *Shotgun Boogie* (1950). By 1955 he was an established favorite with mass audiences via network radio shows on CBS and ABC, and had top-selling records including the Kay Starr duet *I'll Never Be Free* (1950), *The Ballad Of Davy Crockett* (1955, the theme from the Walt Disney movie, which was also cut – and became a Top 5 hit – by the picture's star Fess Parker), and *Sixteen Tons* (1955, the famed coal-mining song penned by Merle Travis). The last named became the singer's biggest success and remained in the charts for six months as well as selling more than four-million copies over the following ten years. Ford subsequently gained his own NBC television show and, although he scored a dozen or so more hits, his role within country became more that of 'elder statesman' taking key roles in such events as the early CMA Award Shows. These days he mainly concerns himself with gospel recordings.

In 1950 Capitol's country duties were taken over by Ken Nelson and the roster steadily built by Hank Thompson, Faron Young, Ferlin Husky, Jean Shepard, Wanda Jackson and Sonny James, as well as being the obvious label outlet for the West Coast artists themselves.

One of the local catches was Buck Owens, a singer who not only was one of Capitol's – and country's biggest successes of the 1960s (he scored nearly four-dozen hits during the decade) but was also the catalyst for the development of the West Coast country scene. His headquarters were based in Bakersfield, a township of 60,000 population in a rich farming and oil-producing area some 115 miles north of Los Angeles. It was also the home of Tommy Collins, Merle Haggard, Billy Mize, Red Simpson and Kay Adams, as well as others more locally known, while Owens' wife Bonnie also scored some success as a recording artist. It had a number of country nightspots and radio stations pumping out the music; one of its earliest deejays was Ferlin Husky.

By the mid-1960s the town was a thriving country center, attracting the enthusiasm of fans who wanted the more solid, traditional approach (rather than the poppified Nashville Sound) and had earned itself the title 'Nashville West,' though many of the West Coast then regarded Nashville as 'Bakersfield East.' But, to others, there was a title that drove home its message directly – 'Buckersfield.'

Bakersfield had already established a minor reputation prior to Owens' emergence, with Tommy Collins moving there from

***Left and above:* Tennessee Ernie Ford earned his success on radio and television and today concentrates on recording gospel music.**
***Top:* Buck Owens surrounded by his band, The Buckaroos. In 1965 he vowed to sing only country music.**

Oklahoma City on the strength of a Capitol deal. He established national attention with a succession of uptempo, novelty recordings that included *You Better Not Do That* (1954), *Whatcha Gonna Do Now* (1954) and *It Tickles* (1955). His stature was further increased by his songwriting output which, by the late 1960s, totaled some 800 songs. His other big hit was another novelty *If You Can't Bite, Don't Growl* (1966, for Columbia), and he was afforded a beautiful tribute in *Leonard* (making use of his real name, Leonard Raymond Sipes), penned and recorded by Merle Haggard. Collins had also employed Owens as a guitarist in his band as well as using him on several early records.

Buck Owens (born Sherman, Texas, 12 August 1929) spent his teenage years hauling goods between Arizona and California's San Joaquin Valley and had settled in Bakersfield by the time he was 21. It was his skills as a guitarist, working sessions for such as Sonny James, Faron Young, Wanda Jackson and the aforementioned Collins, together with his songwriting talents, that caught the attention of the Capitol executives and gained him his own recording contract in 1956. But another three years passed before he made his brief chart debut with *Second Fiddle,* though the next, *Under Your Spell Again,* was there for nearly half a year. *Above And Beyond* and *Excuse Me (I Think I Got A Heartache)* followed in 1960 and, by 1963, he was holding down the top spot with such as *Act Naturally* (later to be recorded by the Beatles) and *Love's Gonna Live Here*; in 1964 *My Heart Skips A Beat, Together Again* and *I Don't Care* all succeeded. A year later he broke further ground by taking *I've Got A Tiger By The Tail* into the pop charts.

Owens' music comprised honky-tonk styling with shades of western swing, put over by his high tenor voice and heavy instrumentation (on many recordings, by his band, The Buckaroos). Many of the songs were uptempo and kept to barroom and love themes and delighted those country fans not too pleased with the watered-down sounds then stemming from Nashville. He further secured his relationship with these followers by taking a full page advertisement in the trade journals during spring 1965 for his 'Pledge to Country Music' which, among other items, stated that he was 'proud to be associated with country music' and that he 'would not sing any song that wasn't a country song.' The remainder of the decade saw more Number 1s with *Open Up Your Heart* (1966), *Sam's Place* (1967) and *How Long Will My Baby Be Gone* (1968), though one might well have thought twice about that pledge as he stormed the heights with Chuck Berry's *Johnny B. Goode* (1969) and Simon & Garfunkel's *Bridge Over Troubled Waters* (1972).

The 1970s saw his recording career trailing off – though he made the Top 10 duetting with Emmylou Harris on *Play Together Again* (1979, on Warner Bros), but he still continues to retain his popularity as one of the stalwart hosts on television's most successful country show Hee Haw.

Another prominent member of the Bakersfield clan was Missouri-born Wynn Stewart who, after securing a number of local hits on the Challenge label, broke into the bigtime with *Wishful Thinkin'* (1959). He signed with Capitol in 1964 and, three years later, went to the top with the attractive *It's Such A Pretty World Today.* By that time he had departed from Bakersfield and cut down on his road work, more content to headline at his own Nashville-Nevada Club in Las Vegas. Besides contributing a number of very pleasing (and, commercially, underrated) songs to the world of country, Stewart also gave employment to a young musician destined to dethrone Owens as 'the king of Bakersfield.' His name was Merle Haggard.

Strangely, Haggard was one of the few California-based country singers who was actually born in the state (born Oakdale, 6 April 1937), the son of migrant parents who were victims of Oklahoma's Dust Bowl droughts. His early life and clashes with the law – which, by the time of his 23rd birthday, had mounted to seven years in reform schools and a three-year stretch at San Quentin – have been much written about and detailed in the singer's autobiography *Sing Me Back Home.* Finally paroled in 1960, he settled in Bakersfield and worked as a ditchdigger while moonlighting as a guitarist in the town's rough-and-tumble nightclub area, known locally as 'beer can hill.' After working in Stewart's band and gaining initial help from Owens and his wife Bonnie (whom Haggard later married, undoubtedly adding to the friction that later built between the two singers as Owens noted the other's rapidly growing popularity), he was discovered by Charles 'Fuzzy' Owens and Lewis Tally, leading on to recording for the small Tally label

and his chart debut with a Wynn Stewart composition, *Sing A Sad Song* (1963). A couple of years later he broke into the Top 10 with *(My Friends Are Gonna Be) Strangers,* penned by Nashville-writer Liz Anderson, which led on to a new recording deal with Capitol. At this stage Haggard started recording his own songs, which centered on traditional themes of prison, barrooms and family. The cycle started rolling with *Swingin' Doors* (1966) and *The Bottle Let Me Down* (1966), and secured his first Number 1 with *I'm A Lonesome Fugitive* (1966). By 1970 he had another seven chart toppers under his belt – including *Branded Man* (1967), *Sing Me Back Home* (1967) and *Mama Tried* (1968) – and had become something of a national personality with *Okie From Muskogee* (1969), a song that spoke up for the silent majority in the troubled times of Vietnam but one that Merle later admitted was tongue-in-cheek. Nevertheless that didn't stop him flag-waving again with *The Fightin' Side Of Me* (1970), though he then moved into safer territories with Ernest Tubb's *Soldier's Last Letter* (1971) and Tommy Collins *Carolyn* (1971).

His music showed that he was a writer of considerable perception, sensitivity and originality and to these qualities he added the role of musical historian by recording tribute albums to two of his, and country music's, greatest influences – Jimmie Rodgers (*Same Train, A Different Time,* 1969) and Bob Wills (*A Tribute To The Best Damn Fiddle Player In The World,* 1970). In 1973 he brought another ambitious project to fruition, a double album entitled *A Land Of Many Churches* which provided a musical documentary view of gospel worship in contemporary America, using the Carter Family on a number of the tracks. His other concept albums have included *I Love Dixie Blues* (1974), a live concert album with Dixieland as a major musical theme; *My Love Affair With Trains* (1976), spot-lighting his interest in trains; and, after a move to MCA, a hastily assembled tribute to Presley, *My Farewell To Elvis* (1977). Meanwhile the hit singles kept flowing and included *Grandma Harp* (1972), *If We Make It Through December* (1973, which also put him in the pop charts) and *Cherokee Maiden* (1976), a revival of a Bob Wills' song. By the 1980s he had charted over 50 singles (more than half of them Number 1's) and was set to begin a new recording era, this time with Epic, that commenced with the fine-sounding *Big City* (1982). He also recorded an outstanding album with Willie Nelson, *Poncho And Lefty,* which displayed the two artists' common interest in musical heritage, and deservedly won the 1983 CMA Album of the Year Award.

Country-music fans have always remained loyal to Haggard, respecting his musical integrity and lack of compromise to current trends, ingredients that are realized through both his recordings and stage performances with his band, The Strangers. The outfit sometimes numbers a dozen musicians and incorporates wife Leona Williams (a recording artist for around 15 years) and former Texas Playboys.

But Bakersfield didn't wholly dominate the West Coast country scene, though Capitol Records in Los Angeles was certainly keeping a check on the talent. During the early 1960s two musicians were beginning careers that would eventually make them superstars. Their names were Glen Campbell and Roy Clark.

Glen Campbell (born Delight, Arkansas, 22 April 1936), the seventh son of a seventh son who learned to play guitar by the age of six, built his reputation as one of Hollywood's busiest musicians. He started performing in his uncle Dick Bills' western band, prior to getting together his own group in New Mexico, and had a minor hit record with *Turn Around, Look At Me* (1961) on the small Crest

Left: **Merle Haggard, reliving the sound of western swing. He owns a fiddle that was pased on to him by Bob Wills.**

Above: **Tommy Collins wrote about 800 songs within 20 years.**
Top: **Wynn Stewart headlined at his own Nashville-Nevada Club.**

Above (left to right): **Johnny Cash with Roy Clark, June Carter Cash and Tony Orlando, who appeared on the Johnny Cash Christmas Special that was taped in and around Nashville.**
Left: **Merle Haggard has a loyal following. He was a talented songwriter; many of his hits were his own compositions.**

label. Capitol signed him and he charted with *Kentucky Means Paradise* (1962), but another four years were to pass before real action came his way.

In the meantime his guitar work was gaining him more and more studio sessions, backing such as The Beach Boys (with whom he briefly worked on the road), Jan and Dean, Rick Nelson, Frank Sinatra, Elvis Presley and the Mamas and the Papas. One year he worked a staggering 586 sessions which, as he noted, only brought forth three hits – an observation that led him to start analyzing his own recordings and to start doing his recordings his own way.

In 1967 he scored a Top 30 hit with *Gentle On My Mind* (penned by John Hartford and probably the most recorded song in country-music history), followed by *By The Time I Get To The Phoenix*, the first of a batch of Jimmy Webb songs that would make the singer a superstar. *Wichita Lineman* (1968), *Galveston* (1969) and *Where's The Playground, Susie* (1969) followed and, in the wake of their country and pop-chart appearances, he secured his own network television series and starring roles in the Paramount movies *True Grit* and *Norwood.*

Campbell succeeded with a sound that went further than that being produced in Nashville, making full use of orchestras and vocal choruses and geared directly toward the pop market. But, then, he didn't care for categorizations and stated that there were only two kinds of music, 'good and bad.' The success continued and, besides cutting some duets with Bobbie Gentry and Anne Murray, he stormed the charts with *It's Only Make Believe* (1970), *Rhinestone Cowboy* (1975) and *Southern Nights* (1977) before finally leaving Capitol and signing a new deal with Atlantic-America in 1982. He's also built up considerable popularity overseas, especially in Britain where he's been staging sell-out tours since April 1973. His other achievements include being named CMA Entertainer of the Year in 1968 and the establishment of the Glen Campbell Los Angeles Open, a major event in golfing circles.

Roy Clark (born Meherrin, Virginia, 15 April 1933) was also named CMA Entertainer, in 1973, the title being afforded him

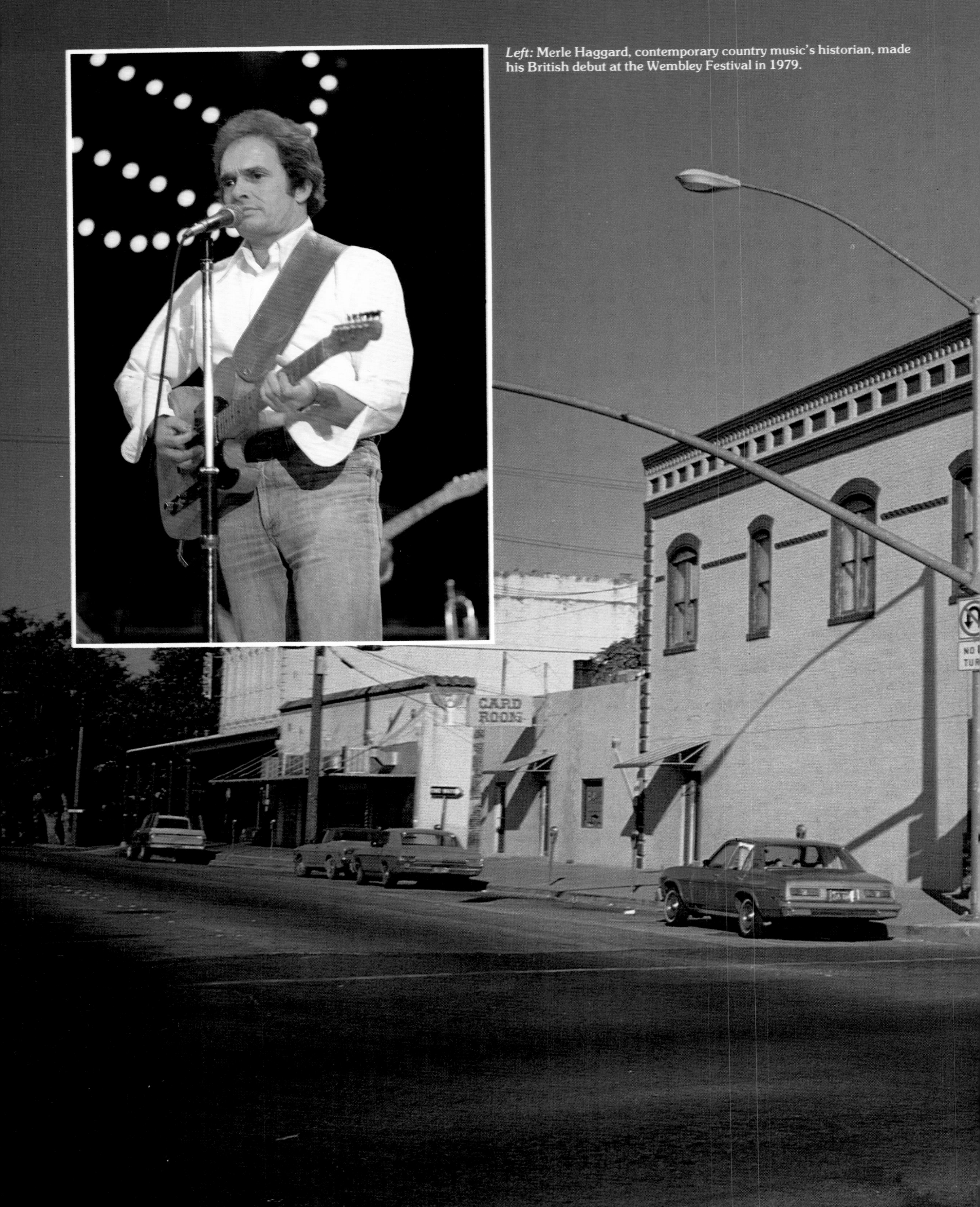

Left: Merle Haggard, contemporary country music's historian, made his British debut at the Wembley Festival in 1979.

Below: This typical western saloon is located in Red Bluff, California, just down Interstate 5 from Redding, where Merle Haggard lives today.

Left and inset: Although he achieved international success as a sing
Glen Campbell still devotes a lot of his stage time to guitar work

Above, all four: **Glen Campbell became a superstar recording artist in the late 1960s singing songs by John Hartford and Jimmy Webb. A recent development of his many talents incorporates the bagpipes in his music. In the photograph second from the top he is shown performing in London.**

because of his skills as an instrumentalist, singer and comedian – talents that have led him to be cited 'the compleat entertainer' by virtually all the US major variety critics. The son of a guitar-playing tobacco farmer, he had won the National Country Music Banjo championship by the late 1940s and began 'paying his dues' by landing spots on Jimmy Dean's ABC network television series. As a member of George Hamilton IV's television series, he earned a place in Wanda Jackson's band – and it was through the encouragement of this singer, and Hank Thompson, that he came to the attention of Capitol Records (after making singles for labels like Four Star, Debbie and Carol). He made his chart debut with *Tips Of My Fingers* (1963).

Throughout the 1960s he was much in demand as a guitarist as well as making many television appearances – which included showing off his comedy skills with double guest spots on The Beverly Hillbillies (1962-71) as Cousin Roy and his mother, Big Mama Halsey (named after his manager and business associate, Jim Halsey) – and winning ecstatic audience applause in the Las Vegas nightspots. Then came 1969, a momentous year, as he broke through to the country-pop market with a sensitive handling of Charles Aznavour's *Yesterday When I Was Young* (one of the first releases following his move to Dot Records) and the beginning of the lengthy association with television's Hee Haw series.

Clark has never repeated the success of the 1969 single, but he has achieved substantial country hits with *Thank God And Greyhound* (1970), *Come Live With Me* (1973) and *If I Had It To Do All Over Again* (1976), as well as releasing many vocal and guitar albums, including teamings with banjoist sidekick Buck Trent, legendary blues' master Clarence 'Gatemouth' Brown and a loving roots album with his kinfolk (*Family Album*, 1973). The range of his material is vast, moving from bluegrass sessions to Spanish titles, from country standards to Kurt Weill's *September Song* (1969). Sadly none of his recordings puts over the entertainer's sheer versatility, which made him one of country music's biggest money earners in recent years.

The West Coast also created its own trade organization, the Academy of Country and Western Music, formed in 1964 with the aim of best serving the area's growing roster of country artists. Its first president was Tex Williams, who served until 1968 and was succeeded by Johnny Bond. Annual awards were introduced in 1965 and set out to honor musicians as well as the stars.

By the end of the 1960s a new hybrid sound had become a vital part of Los Angeles' musical landscape, country-rock, born out of

Above, all three: Roy Clark, the son of a guitar-playing tobacco farmer, has been dubbed 'the compleat entertainer' for his abilities as a guitarist, singer and comedian. He has produced a large number of recordings but his versatility can be best appreciated during live shows. *Next page:* The Dillards, innovators or country rock, were the first band to experiment with mixing bluegrass and acoustic music with rock.

Above: Emmylou Harris, whose distinctly clear voice has put her in a country class of her own, is shown here in 1979.

Below: Emmylou Harris' Hot Band, comprising some of the finest talent around, is as famous as the lady herself.

rock musicians' growing desire to broaden their musical horizons. But the blending of the genres had also happened in the other camp, first, as a number of inventive country musicians started to look further afield for inspiration and with a desire to capture the attention of the youth market.

The Dillards – a bluegrass group from Missouri who moved to Los Angeles, and comprising brothers Doug (banjo) and Rodney Dillard (guitar, dobro) and friends Mitch Jayne (bass) and Dean Webb (mandolin), were among the first to experiment and receive nationwide recognition for their free-ranging bluegrass sounds. They secured a deal with Elektra Records (at the time run by Jac Holzman as an outlet for prestigious folk acts) and made their album debut with *Back Porch Bluegrass* (1963). By the time of their classic *Wheatstraw Suite* (1968) album, the group's horizons had broadened, with their close-harmony working material by such as Lennon & McCartney, Tim Hardin and Herb Pedersen (the last named, one of LA's influential country-rock musicians, was now working with the group, having taken the place of Rodney Dillard). The group's greatest achievement, though, was presenting acoustic instruments in entirely fresh surroundings. Another Elektra album of the period successfully combined the musical realms of bluegrass and pop/rock music. Recorded by New England's Charles River Valley Boys, *Beatle Country* featured entirely the music of John Lennon and Paul McCartney.

Other West Coast-based, bluegrass bands that attracted the attention of rock audiences included The Kentucky Colonels – which was headlined by brothers Clarence (guitar) and Roland White (mandolin) – and Country Gazette which featured the skills of Byron Berline (multiawarded champion fiddle player, who proved an innovative force in the country-rock movement), Roger Bush (string bass), Kenny Wertz (guitar, vocals), Alan Munde (banjo, vocals) and, again, Roland White. Such groups won the appreciation of rock audiences as well as finding a ready market in folk circles and on college campuses.

The person who firmly established the identity of country-rock was Gram Parsons (born Winter Haven, Florida, 5 November 1946), who was raised on country music in Georgia, and his interest in it reawakened during his brief four months at Harvard University. In the next six years, and with short associations with a number of groups and musicians, he became the new music's most influential figure.

It started with the International Submarine Band in Los Angeles in 1967, a group that lasted long enough for an album to be produced on Lee Hazelwood's LHI Records (*Safe At Home*) before cult rock band The Byrds, who had touched upon country in some of their recordings, got hold of Parsons. He stayed with the group (that featured Roger McGuinn, Chris Hillman and Kevin Kelley) for only three months, but that was long enough to bring the music full circle and for Parsons to be the influential force on the definitive country-rock album, *Sweetheart Of The Rodeo* (1968). By the end of the year he had formed another band, The Flying Burrito Brothers, with Hillman, Chris Ethridge and steel-guitarist 'Sneeky' Pete Kleinow.

Parsons stayed with the Burritos long enough to record *The Gilden Palace Of Sin* album (1969, A&M Records) and play such country venues as LA's Palomino Club while working out the musical directions that suited him best. This came together with the assistance of such as guitarist James Burton, pianist Glen D Hardin and fiddle-player Byron Berline, as well as a talented, sweet-voiced unknown, Emmylou Harris. The results were heard on *G.P.* (1973), an album that paid an honest-to-goodness tribute to the basic roots of country. The next move was to get his newly formed Fallen Angel Band on the road, but his wishes were hardly fulfilled. He died on 19 September 1973, the cause of death apparently being a heart attack. Many people noted that he had gone the way of other country legends, 'living hard, dying young.' A second solo album, *Grievous Angel*, was released shortly afterward.

***Above and top:* Emmylou Harris was unsuccessful as a folk singer but made her mark in country music.**

While Parsons did not live to realize the results of his endeavors, he had helped introduce Emmylou Harris, who not only secured a recording contract with Warner Bros. but also had readymade one of the most prestigious groupings of musicians in the business which she named, appropriately, The Hot Band. Born in Birming-

Left and next page: **Linda Rondstadt emerged from her folk beginnings in the 1960s to become a leader of the 1970s country-rock movement. Her success stretches right across the entertainment field, and has brought country music to a large new audience.**

ham, Alabama (2 April 1949), she says she 'didn't get turned on to country until later in my life, but obviously it was there.' She had tried her luck as a folk singer, had the doors shut in her face in Nashville and eventually met her mentor in Washington. It was Parsons who turned her on to the music of the Louvin Brothers, the early country songs of the Everly Brothers and the material of Felice and Boudleaux Bryant, though the lady later discovered – and became an addict of – the music of George Jones. She released her debut album *Pieces Of The Sky* (1975) to high critical acclaim, and received a high chart placing for her second single, the Louvins' *If I Could Only Win Your Love*, a song that perfectly recaptured the plaintiveness of country's traditional past. By 1976 she was at the top of the country charts with country standards – Buck Owens' *Together Again* and Don Gibson's *Sweet Dreams* – and started moving toward more contemporary material, though retaining a country feel, with songs such as *Two More Bottles Of Wine* (1978, penned by one-time Hot Band member, Rodney Crowell). Strangely, although she received adoration from both country and rock markets, it wasn't until 1981 that she made her debut in the pop charts, with a revival of *Mr. Sandman*.

Emmylou Harris' output of albums have kept mainly to country, with *Blue Kentucky Girl* (1979) well entrenched in country roots (and providing good reason for her collecting the CMA Female Vocalist award) and *Roses In The Snow* (1980) paying loving homage to bluegrass. She was an artist whose music ran against the grain for, while the mainstream industry battled for crossover success, she proudly waved the flag on behalf of tradition. She made her intentions even clearer in 1983 by uprooting herself from Los Angeles and moving to Nashville.

The other important singer to emerge from the Los Angeles scene was Linda Ronstadt (born Tucson, Arizona, 15 July 1946) who, like Harris, started her career in 'folksy' surroundings. She was a member of the Stone Poneys, achieving one big hit *Different Drum* in 1967, before commencing a solo career on Capitol which, although directed at a rock market, was heavily infiltrated with country. In fact her second album, *Linda Ronstadt* (1970) was recorded in Nashville. It wasn't until four years later that she began making impressions with country devotees *en masse*. Her version of Hank Williams' *I Can't Help It* (1975) just missed the top of the charts and her version of Phil Everly's *When Will I Be Loved* (1975) was one of the most played records of the year. Other big country successes included *Love Is A Rose* (1975), *Crazy* (1976) and *Blue Bayou* (1977), though by the end of the decade she had emerged as one of the biggest attractions on the rock scene. She displayed a versatility that would later see her appearing on Broadway in Gilbert & Sullivan's *Pirates Of Penzance* and recording an album of pop standards with the Nelson Riddle Orchestra (*What's New*, 1983). Nevertheless she has helped bring country to audiences who, otherwise, might have given it a miss, while endearing herself to the country market through a succession of hit singles and a close friendship with Dolly Parton and Emmylou Harris.

By the mid-1970s the movement that had started with Gram Parsons had developed and seen the creation of bands like New Riders Of The Purple Sage, Poco, the Ozark Mountain Daredevils and the biggest country-rock supergroup of them all, The Eagles, although such groups should be discussed in rock publications. On the other hand, the hard core country movement was being wound down, with singers like Buck Owens and Merle Haggard tying closer binds to Nashville, as did the country divisions of the West Coast-based Capitol and Warner Bros. record labels.

Crossover and Controversy

'Twin fiddles don't make it country anymore – and *not* having twin fiddles doesn't make it *not* country. Country is no longer the basic sound anymore than rock 'n' roll is. Country is really a state of mind.' Thus spoke Billy Sherrill, country music's main hit record producer of recent years, though many country fans were to wonder whether he was really producing country or yet another hybrid, this time closely related to pop music itself.

The 1970s saw the ultimate broadening of the music, leading on to country's biggest boom period ever. Anything, it seemed, was fair game if hits were the end result. Another pacemaker, Kris Kristofferson, offered his own explanation. He put it simply, 'if it sounds country, it is.'

It was a decade of innovation and experimentation, expanding careers and country-pop success, breaking new grounds and heated controversy. It was also the decade that put a new word on everybody's lips – crossover. It meant exactly what it said – a music crossing from one area and meeting success in another. In the case of country, it meant reaping the rewards of success in the pop charts. Crossover was the name of the game in the 1970s and, once one or two records hit the pop charts, very few producers were content to let their ambitions rest with just country laurels. Big success meant big dollars and the country industry started gearing itself to win in the profitable pop market, with productions that grew bigger, more lavish and far more costly. Whereas the Nashville Sound presented a smoother approach to country, this new movement frequently adopted itself to the strains of pop.

As the lines between country and pop/rock grew closer together, so controversy started to rage. Radio stations first brought the music to the attention of many cosmopolitan listeners, an audience that thought the music 'hick and hillbilly.' The strength of country programing is asserted by figures. In 1971 there were 525 stations presenting country full time, 1116 in 1975 and 1534 in 1980, or 2403 if radio stations that partially programmed it are also taken into consideration. Many of the stations that switched to country were originally rock, and many of the deejays were originally 'rock jocks' and their tastes were somewhat different from those who had worked a lifetime in country radio. Hence the greater programing of pop/rock-styled country (which, sometimes, didn't even include bona fide country singers) and the beginning of the controversy.

The 1970s began quietly enough, with country getting a boost as the husband-and-wife team of Jack Blanchard and Misty Morgan made the charts with the novelty *Tennessee Bird Walk* (1970) and, the next year, Alabama-born ex-marine Freddie Hart arrived with *Easy Loving*. This was to be this singer/songwriter's greatest triumph, for the record not only remained a country hit for 24 weeks but also set a precedent at the CMA Awards by winning the Song of the Year accolade for two consecutive years. Hart followed up with a song that was his catch phrase, *Bless Your Heart* (1972).

The singles that set the trends were Lynn Anderson's *Rose Garden*, and two songs by up-and-coming writer Kris Kristofferson – *Help Me Make It Through The Night* and *For The Good Times*, the first cut by the relative unknown Sammi Smith, the second by top-seller Ray Price. All three were released in 1970 and made strong overtures to the pop market.

Lynn Anderson (born Grand Forks, North Dakota, 26 September 1947) was already well known to country audiences, having made her chart debut on Chart Records with *Ride Ride Ride* (1966), and scoring another fifteen hits – including *Promises Promises* (1967) and *That's A No No* (1969) – before signing with Columbia in 1970. The daughter of songwriters Liz and Casey Anderson, the industry ties were further strengthened as her then-husband was songwriter/producer Glenn Sutton. It was Sutton who produced *Rose Garden*, penned by Joe South, and added swirling strings arranged by Cam Mullins and full-bodied choruses from the Nashville Edition, resulting in a million-selling country-pop smash and securing his wife the 1971 CMA Female Vocalist award. She followed up with more country Number 1s such as *You're My Man* (1971), *Keep Me In Mind* (1973) and *What A Man My Man Is* (1974), though during the second part of the decade went into semiretirement to pursue the roles of housewife and mother. In 1983 she started a comeback by signing with Dallas' Permian Records.

California-born, though Nashville-based, Sammi Smith was never able to match the success of her two-million selling, CMA awarded *Help Me Make It Through The Night*, though her husky-styled vocals and poignant phrasing certainly deserved full recognition. She originally achieved a trio of hits on Columbia, but signing to the newly launched Mega label – and recording the Kristofferson-composed song – put her right on top. However, the glories were brief and she only returned to the Top 10 with *Then You Walk In* (1971) and Haggard's *Today I Started Loving You Again* (1975) while she switched between labels and earned herself the reputation of being something of a rebel.

Kris Kristofferson was also viewed as a rebel in the eyes of the Nashville industry, though the walls started crumbling down in

Right: **One-time Rhodes Scholar Kris Kristofferson became a very successful songwriter, 'opened up' Nashville in 1970 and then became one of Hollywood's hottest properties.**

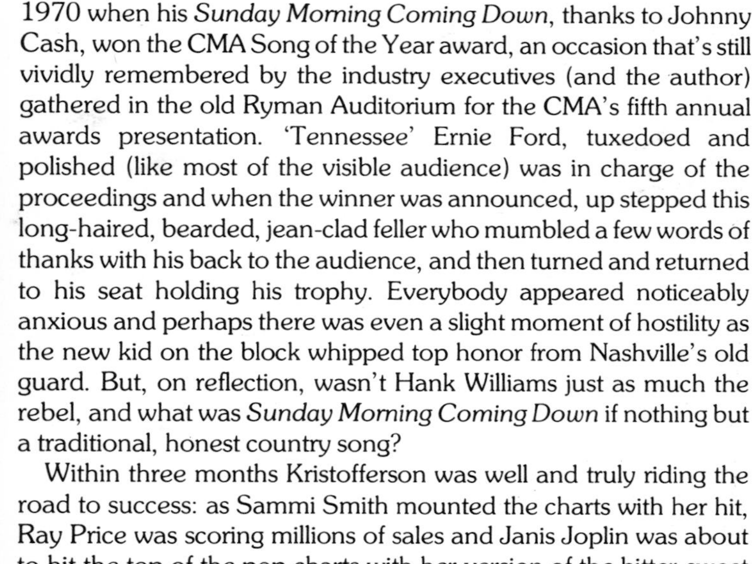

1970 when his *Sunday Morning Coming Down*, thanks to Johnny Cash, won the CMA Song of the Year award, an occasion that's still vividly remembered by the industry executives (and the author) gathered in the old Ryman Auditorium for the CMA's fifth annual awards presentation. 'Tennessee' Ernie Ford, tuxedoed and polished (like most of the visible audience) was in charge of the proceedings and when the winner was announced, up stepped this long-haired, bearded, jean-clad feller who mumbled a few words of thanks with his back to the audience, and then turned and returned to his seat holding his trophy. Everybody appeared noticeably anxious and perhaps there was even a slight moment of hostility as the new kid on the block whipped top honor from Nashville's old guard. But, on reflection, wasn't Hank Williams just as much the rebel, and what was *Sunday Morning Coming Down* if nothing but a traditional, honest country song?

Within three months Kristofferson was well and truly riding the road to success: as Sammi Smith mounted the charts with her hit, Ray Price was scoring millions of sales and Janis Joplin was about to hit the top of the pop charts with her version of the bitter-sweet *Me And Bobby McGee* (1972).

Born in Brownsville, Texas (22 June 1936), the son of an Air Force Major General, Kristofferson had arrived in Nashville just about the time that Roger Miller was shaking the foundations with his unorthodox approach to country lyrics. He had come to town with a Harvard Rhodes scholarship behind him, a discontinued career as a novelist and the first stab at recording (in England, using the name Kris Carson, while studying at Oxford University). He had then spent time with the Army in Germany, where he played service clubs and started writing songs. It wasn't easy at first in Nashville and he spent his time between jobs like janitoring at Columbia studios and flying helicopters out to the oil rigs in the Gulf of Mexico struggling to get his songs heard. Writer/publisher Marijohn Wilken (with whom he co-wrote *One Day At A Time* in 1973) was among the first to take notice, and the first artists to cut a Kristofferson song were Dave Dudley (*Vietnam Blues*, 1966), Roy Drusky (*Jody And The Kid*, 1968) and Roger Miller, who took three of them (*Darby's Castle, Casey's Last Ride* and the original version of *Me And Bobby McGee*, 1969). Following Cash's cut of *Sunday Morning Coming Down*, Kristofferson took another step forward when Waylon Jennings made a Top 5 hit out of *The Taker* (1970) and Ray Price added the final seal of approval. Suddenly Kristofferson was very much in demand as a writer.

In 1970 he was launched on his own recording career by another long-time supporter, Fred Foster of Monument Records, and he made his album debut with *Kristofferson* (later to be reissued as *Me And Bobby McGee*). He broke into the singles charts a couple of years later with *Loving Her Was Easier (Than Anything I'll Ever Do Again)* and, in 1973, racked up Gold Discs for the chart-topping single *Why Me* and the album *Silver Tongued Devil And I.* Although he continued to record, little matched those early years of creativity, his greatest success coming in the form of country duets with his one-time wife Rita Coolidge. By this time most of his energies were being diverted to his highly successful movie career, to be discussed later.

As far as country was concerned, Kristofferson brought the music into the 1970s by broadening its lyrics with a contemporary literacy that made them appealing to mass audiences though hardly swaying from basic country themes. Such endeavors helped the cause of other rebels like Waylon Jennings and Willie Nelson a few years later, though its most immediate effect was to turn the spotlight on other new writers offering a fresh perception to country.

***Left, all three:* Kris Kristofferson in concert with his one-time wife, Rita Coolidge, and Billy Swann in 1975.**

Among these were Mickey Newbury, who scored a major triumph with *An American Trilogy* (1971); Eddie Rabbitt, later to become a crossover superstar; and Chris Gantry, who had already notched up success as Glen Campbell recorded his *Dreams Of The Everyday Housewife* (1968). A cameraderie existed, explains Gantry, that could be liken to that of the impressionists in Paris several decades earlier. He recalls:

> We all hung out together in the streets for a lot of years and saw each other every day. We used to compare our songs and went through the whole cameraderie that exists between songwriters, like a very exclusive sort of life. It was like an apprenticeship because we were around some very heavy writers and we all influenced each other because we were all different. The Nashville industry didn't go too much for it at first, and it took us a long time to be even accepted to the point when somebody would even consider recording one of our songs. Then when we did start getting some cuts, they jumped on us as being 'the new breed' though we'd actually been there for a long time.

The songwriters provided one aspect of the crossover movement, the record producers another. Here Billy Sherrill enters the picture. He had already established his Nashville reputation in the 1960s as record producer and songwriter, and was the person responsible for the success of Tammy Wynette and David Houston. His musical connections went back much further and began in his home state of Alabama, where he cut his teeth playing piano at his father's evangelist meetings and, later, as a saxophonist in local rock 'n' roll bands. He gained studio knowledge with Sam Phillips at Sun Records where, besides engineering such as Jerry Lee Lewis' *What I'd Say* (1961), he achieved his own small slice of fame with *Tipsy*, a saxophone instrumental which he wrote, produced and recorded. In 1966 he first made his mark in country music when, as a producer for the fledgling Epic label (a division of CBS), he cut a session with David Houston which resulted in *Almost Persuaded* being flipped from a 'B' support song to an 'A' side million seller. From that point on, Sherrill began breaking rules in the country recording book.

The secret of Billy Sherrill's success lay not in pursuing the established Nashville Sound but, rather, creating records that sounded different. At first, with artists like Houston and Wynette, he made the presentation very country, but in the 1970s his approach veered more toward middle-of-the-road music with the premise that, everytime he stepped into a studio, he was there to create a hit single. A hit album would follow later, its strength resting upon the success of the single. In the late 1970s, while holding down the post of Vice President/Executive Producer, CBS Records, he remarked:

> There have been a lot of changes during the past 15 years. Just over a decade ago there were maybe a dozen artists who cornered the country market and everything they recorded sold well. But the pendulum has swung from the name to the material, and today the market is much larger.

Sherrill was both the discoverer of talent and the regenerator of careers. His first major find of the 1970s was a 13-year-old girl from Seminole, Texas, named Tanya Tucker (born 10 October 1958) whose father yearned for her, and her sister LaCosta, to find success in the music business. For several years the family moved around the country, chasing stars, entering talent contests, auditioning and cutting demo tapes. The break came when some of the youngster's demos arrived on Sherrill's desk; he was impressed enough to track her to Las Vegas, fly out and consummate a deal. A

Left: Charlie Rich, 'The Silver Fox,' blends rhythm 'n' blues, jazz and country to achieve million-sales success.
Above: Lynn Anderson had her first hit record in the mid-1960s, succeeded by several more over the next ten years.

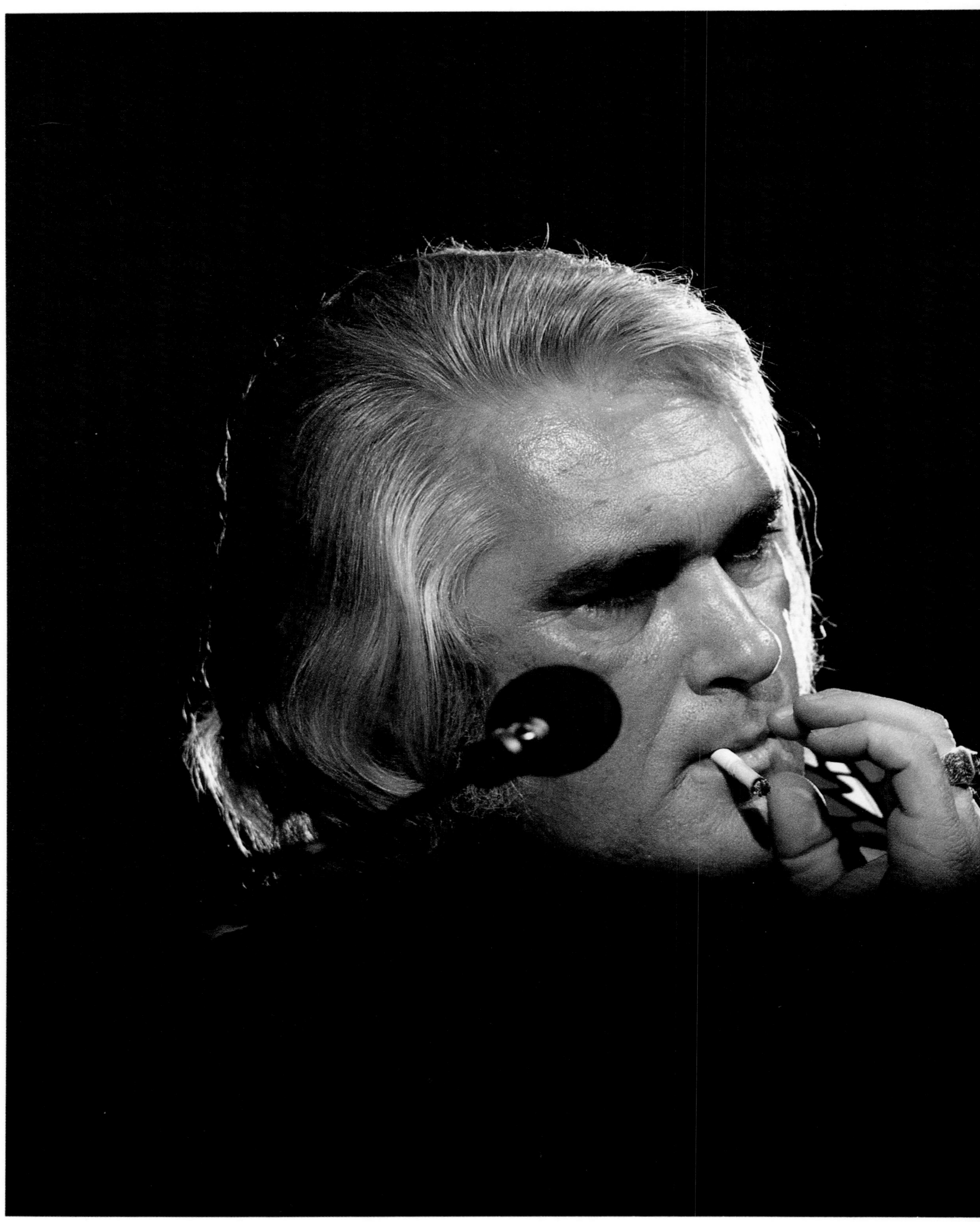

Far left: **Charlie Rich started with Sun Records in the late 1950s but his greatest success came two decades later with a string of million sellers.**
Below left: **A prodigy at thirteen, Johnny Paycheck startled some fans with his lyrics. His voice was rich and versatile.**
Left: **Tanya Tucker had her first break at age thirteen.**

month or so later she was in Columbia's Nashville studios cutting *Delta Dawn,* penned by Alex Harvey, a song that the producer considered ideal for her. By mid-1972 it was racing up the charts and creating a positive, if startled, reaction from audiences. Tanya Tucker had arrived. More important, Tanya Tucker had arrived with an image of teenager singing provocative lyrics, though her powerful voice hardly gave any indication of her tender years. Sherrill then further developed his 'wayfaring child' with songs of a similar ilk that included *What's Your Mama's Name* (1973), *Would You Lay With Me (In A Field Of Stone)* (1974) and *The Man That Turned My Mama On* (1974), the total success seeing the young lady moving over to MCA Records in 1975 and signed a contract, on her sixteenth birthday, reputedly worth $1 million. The new era began brightly enough with a couple more chart toppers – *Lizzie And The Rainman* (1975), which also broke into the pop charts, and *San Antone Stroll* (1975) – but sadly the image and Sherrill's guiding hand were gone and the momentum lost, and the singer finally sought new directions by drifting into rock.

Sherrill also worked wonders with established talents, often adding fresh impetus to long-reigning careers, as was the case with George Jones whom he brought to Epic in 1971. He was also responsible for bringing Johnny Paycheck (born Greenfield, Ohio, 31 May 1941) back into the limelight after his career had hit rock bottom as the result of alcoholism and bad management. A decade earlier the singer had gained something of a cult reputation, having first played in the bands of Porter Wagoner, Faron Young, George Jones and Ray Price as well as writing hits for such as Tammy Wynette (*Apartment No 9,* 1966, the singer's first chart entry) and Price (*Touch My Heart,* 1966). He had also cut some rockabilly sides for Decca, under the title of Donny Young, before the Paycheck name rose to attention on the Little Darlin' logo. Hits like *The Lovin' Machine* (1966) and *Jukebox Charlie* (1967) won audiences with a voice that carried an incredible vocal range. Undoubtedly it was such assets that attracted Sherrill, and he brought the singer back into chart territories with *She's All I Got* (1971). In 1977 he achieved his biggest smash with the David Allan Coe-penned *Take This Job And Shove It,* a song that immediately hit home with the blue-collar workers and later inspired a movie. Sadly Paycheck couldn't handle his refound success and by 1983, with drug charges and bankruptcy hovering, the recording association was over.

Undoubtedly Sherrill's biggest triumph came with singer/pianist Charlie Rich (born Colt, Arkansas 14 December 1932,), the one-time Sun artist who had flirted with country and pop success – *Lonely Weekends* (1960) and *Mohair Sam* (1965) – over the years. Influenced by blues and jazz during his high-school and university days, he formed his first group, The Velvetones, which also featured his wife Margaret as vocalist, while serving with the Air Force. After initially working as a musician at Sun (on sessions with such as Warren Smith and Billy Lee Riley), *Lonely Weekends* gave him his pop chart debut. Then he moved to RCA's Grove label and Mercury before joining forces with Billy Sherrill at Epic in 1968. He immediately started scoring minor country hits like *Raggedy Ann* (1968) and *Nice 'n' Easy* (1970) before moving into the Top 10 with *I Take It On Home* (1972). By this time the producer had formulated his easy-listening approach to country and found that Rich's gentle styling perfectly fitted the mold. Their talents clicked together with *Behind Closed Doors* (1973), written by Kenny O'Dell, and quickly put the singer on the road to amazing success. Over two years the single was to sell some three-million copies, while the follow-up, *The Most Beautiful Girl* (1973) sold two million, and the next *A Very Special Love Song* (1974) a million. By this time Rich was the hottest property on the recording scene and his past efforts, from other labels, began appearing in all manner of repackagings. One of the singles, *There Won't be Anymore,* on RCA, even made the Number 1 spot on the country charts in 1974.

Charlie Rich's career had expanded in all directions. He was commanding fees as high as any pop act, appeared regularly in Las Vegas and collected three CMA awards in 1973, and a couple more the following year, including the prestigious Entertainer trophy. Such success, however, didn't please everyone. The industry's more traditionally minded noted that his music was not what country was all about. They were also concerned that the singer wasn't all that keen to call himself 'country,' an attitude reinforced by his varied musical influences and his success in the pop market. But while most remained reasonably quiet about Rich's success, there was no holding back the outburst of complaint from these quarters when Olivia Newton-John was chosen as the 1974 CMA Female Vocalist. Here was a singer, it was argued, who had no country background or qualifications, merely a string of hits which had proven successful in that marketplace. This English-born, Australian-raised songstress initially hit the British charts with the country songs *Banks Of The Ohio* (1971) and *Take Me Home, Country Roads* (1973) – and started getting her name around in the States with *Let Me Be There, If You Love Me (Left Me Know)* and *I Honestly Love You,* all immaculately produced in London by John Farrar. The records started getting mass airplay which resulted in high country-chart placings in 1974 and she seemed, after all, a natural contender for the award.

Nashville's traditionalists' outcry was heard nationally and, within a few weeks of the CMA presentations, a new organization had come into being. Named the Association of Country Entertainers (ACE) – and comprising membership purely of country performers, with a 'screening' committee made up of Dolly Parton, Hank Snow, Johnny Paycheck, George Morgan, Jimmy C Newman and Tammy Wynette – the main objective was to protect the interests of the basic country-music scene. Later, at its Nashville press conference, another member, Billy Walker, made the point that the Association was concerned that outside interests were completely diluting the music until it reached the point where it would disappear completely. He added, 'we're mainly people who made country music what it is today, trying to protect our business because we see it flaking off in thousands of directions. We're trying to keep it at home.'

ACE's growl was worse than its bite though and, after its initial publicity, little was heard of the Association, while some of its members even started making inroads into the big wide world of crossover music, not least of all Dolly Parton whose career, by the decade's end, was based in Los Angeles, and her music was infiltrated by rock and disco. As for the two main offenders in the ACE controversy, Charlie Rich had seen his greatest days of glory and Olivia Newton-John was to move on to Hollywood and eventual international superstardom. In spite of ACE, 'outsiders' still found a footing in country while many of Nashville's other producers started following Sherrill's lead in gearing their recordings to mass-audience appeal. The crossover movement went from strength to strength.

Canadian-born Anne Murray (born Springhill, Nova Scotia, 20 June 1946), who taught physical education while moonlighting in music, achieved international stardom with the million-selling

Below: **Anne Murray has been successful as a country singer, but her music crosses over into the pop market.**

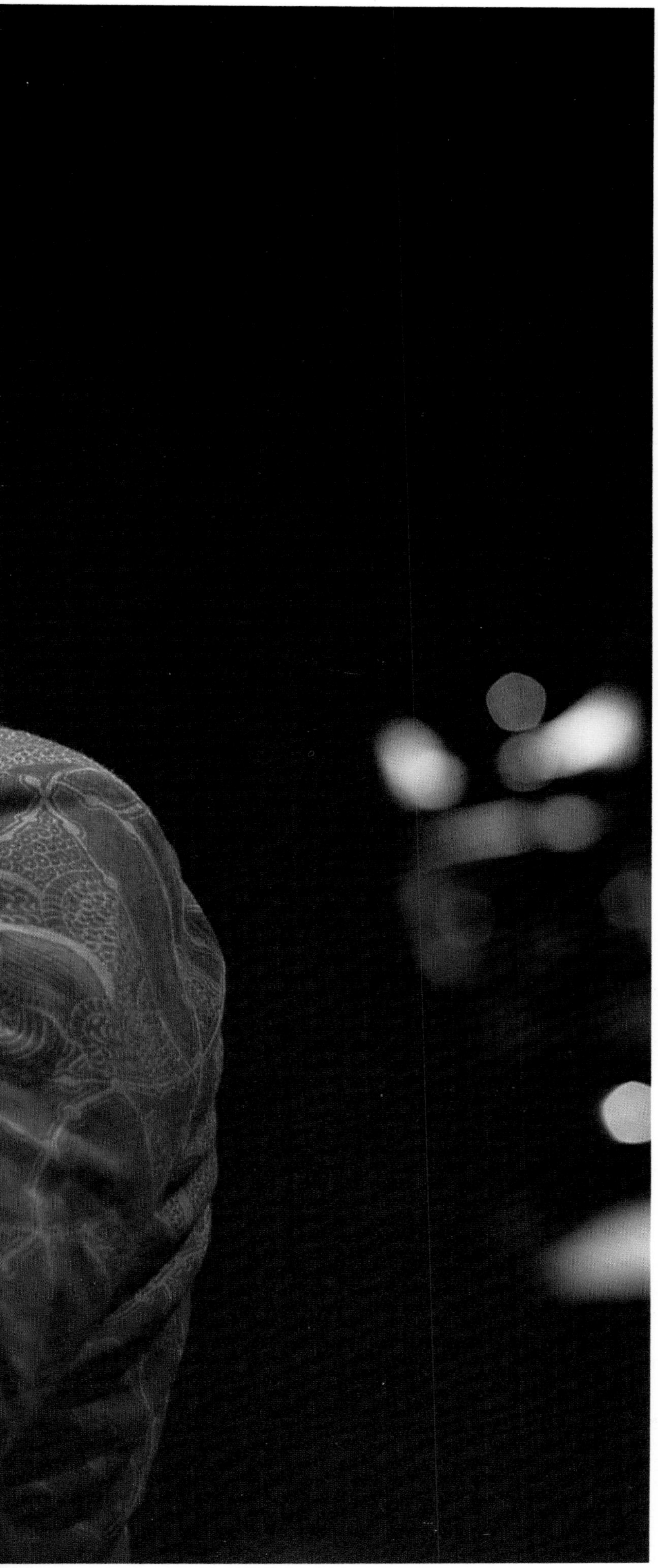

***Above and left:* Colorado-based John Denver is the country boy whose music and success encompasses a broad range of audiences. He became CMA Entertainer of the Year in 1975. His song *Thank God I'm a Country Boy* hit the top of the country charts.**

Snowbird (1970), a local recording produced by Brian Aherne (who would later produce, and marry, Emmylou Harris) that scored heavily in both the country and pop charts. It sounded like a country song and, enhanced by the singer's soft vocals, received considerable country airplay, yet Murray didn't consider herself a country singer. In fact, she knew very little about country music. But it was the country market that was to bring her the greatest success initially. From 1970-78 she had some twenty entries in the country charts (including a revival of George Jones *He Thinks I Still Care,* in 1974), as opposed to four pop entries. Her success as a country singer was determined by the media rather than her own qualifications. In 1978, with the producer's chores taken over by Jim Ed Norman, she moved into superstardom with country-pop (or perhaps pop-country) hits like *You Needed Me* (1978), *I Just Fall In Love Again* (1979), *Broken Hearted Me* (1979), *Daydream Believer* (1980) and *Could I Have This Dance* (1980). Although she's never collected any CMA Awards, she's nevertheless highly thought of by the Nashville community and, in 1983, landed the plum job of co-hosting the Association's annual awards presentation with Willie Nelson.

Another artist not directly related to country music fared even better. In 1975 John Denver (born Roswell, New Mexico, 31 December 1943) walked away with CMA's top accolade, Entertainer of the Year. Although admitting that country was a major influence, his recordings cut across a wide spectrum and also reflect the 1950s rock 'n' roll era and the 1960s folk-music explosion. In spite of his major award, his success in the country music field has been minimal, although his penned *Take Me Home Country*

Above and right: **International superstar Dolly Parton has made her mark on television, in concert and in the movies, and has a steadfast following of country fans.**

Roads (which only got him a Top 50 chart placing in 1971) has been recorded by numerous country singers, as has his *Annie's Song* (1974) and *Back Home Again* (1974). He scored Number 1s with *Thank God I'm A Country Boy* (1975) and *I'm Sorry* (1975), and scored substantial country support again as he dueted with Emmylou Harris on *Wild Mountain Skies* (1983). Overall this Colorado-based entertainer defies categorization and rates as one of the biggest attractions in the whole of show biz.

The most influential factor that decided country music's direction during the 1970s was radio, and, as the number of country stations grew (as program directors found a liking for crossover sounds), they in turn started dictating the kind of music they would feature. *The end result was that they dictated the kind of records that would be featured in the trade papers' charts.* To the numerous stations in the vastly populated metropolitan areas, old-style country music was out. Modern acts, performing the more hybrid style of country, were in, though such directives did bring forth occasional anomalies, like the appearance of artists in the charts who could never be considered remotely country. These included the Pointer Sisters (*Fairytale,* 1975), the Bee Gees (*Rest Your Love On Me,* 1978) and Cher (*It's Too Late To Love Me Now,* 1979), while Britain's Bonnie Tyler and Eric Clapton were among the most played artists in 1978 with *It's A Heartache* and *Lay Down Sally* respectively. Another British singer, Welsh-born Tom Jones, who found international fame by recording *Green Green Grass Of Home* (after hearing Jerry Lee Lewis' version), was regularly featured by a number of country stations, to the effect that his 1983 Mercury recordings were promoted as country. Barbra Streisand and Neil Diamond also gained a chart placing with *You Don't Bring Me Flowers* (1978), though this created a country 'cover' (RCA teamed Jim Ed Brown and Helen Cornelius) which didn't sound that much different in arrangement or instrumentation.

By the mid-1970s all the major record labels had some artists working the crossover route. RCA was no exception, although its one-time country chief, Chet Atkins, had moments of anguish when noting how far the 'sound' had traveled. 'It's changed a lot since I got out of active production, and people have asked me whether I'm sorry I moved the Nashville Sound uptown,' he commented in 1979, 'The answer is yes, in a way, but it had moved such great lengths since I got out of it that I shouldn't have any guilt.' Jerry Bradley, the label's head of Nashville operations during the 1970s, clearly reflected the music's current standing, in particular the influence of radio. In a *Billboard* feature (26 February 1977), he stated that:

> The country deejay is a more progressive, classier type than 10 years ago, particularly in the last four years when a lot of pop stations have lost out on talent to country outlets. The crossover of pop orientated spinners has helped ratings increase as the music changed. They only knew what they were hearing. And while we still have respect for the traditional, we better have a tendency to go where the money is – and that's progressive country today.

Thus the onus for changes has been clearly laid on the line, and sympathy felt for the traditionalists trying to project the music's sound and heritage.

Dolly Parton was the most successful crossover act on RCA, and perfectly illustrated the rags to riches story so commonplace in country, only she achieved far greater heights than most, with her bubbling personality and shrewd business sense contributing to her overall success. The fourth of twelve children born to a mountain family (born Sevier County, Tennessee, 19 January 1946), she was making appearances on Cas Walker's television show in

Knoxville by the age of ten and, three years later, had cut her first record on Louisiana's Goldband label (*Puppy Love,* 1959). She was determined to succeed and, as soon as she graduated from high school in June 1964, she packed her bags and headed west to Nashville, where she started writing songs with her uncle Bill Owens (*Put It Off Until Tomorrow,* a 1966 hit for Bill Phillips was one of their debut successes). Her first record successes came on Monument – *Dumb Blonde* and *Something Fishy,* both in 1967 – and her big break came when she joined Porter Wagoner's television and road show, as well as dueting with him on record. *The Last Thing On My Mind* (1967) started an association that would last six years. They accumulated some twenty duet sucesses and eleven hit albums. Her solo career on RCA commenced in 1968 with *Just Because I'm A Woman* and, within a couple of years, had racked up a Number 1 with *Joshua* (1970). Other big hits, all of which she wrote, included *Coat Of Many Colours* (1971), *My Tennessee Mountain Home* (1973), *Jolene* (1973), *Love Is Like A Butterfly* (1974) and *The Bargain Store* (1975).

Dolly Parton was determined that her music would win out with mass audiences and, coinciding with the release of her 'fresh directions' album *New Harvest, First Gathering* in late 1976, relocated her career in Los Angeles. At the same time she made the statement:

> Any time you make a change, you pay the price. A lot of country people feel I'm leaving the country, that I'm not proud of Nashville, which is the biggest lie there is. I don't want to leave the country, but to take the whole country with me wherever I go.

She quickly established herself in her new surroundings, breaking through to the pop marketplace with *Here You Come Again* (1977), and moving even more toward pop with *Two Doors Down* and *Heartbreaker* (1978). Whatever the country fans might have thought about her musical directions, the industry rewarded her success by naming her CMA Entertainer of the Year in 1978. More varied styles, more Number 1s followed, including the disco-inspired *Baby I'm Burnin'* (1978), a revival of Jerry Lee Lewis rockin' *Great Balls Of Fire* (1979) and the contemporary country *Old Flames (Can't Hold A Candle To You)* (1980). By the beginning of the 1980s, with numerous television appearances and sro concert appearances to her credit, she began another era in a phenomenally successful career by making her movie debut in *9 To 5.*

Dolly Parton achieved what she set out for, to win popularity from mass audiences and, in doing so, has become an international superstar. But she need not have worried about losing country support – the fans have been with her all the way, proving, in some instances, that the boundaries of country be stretched quite considerably. As for the buxom entertainer, she remains proud of her country roots and talks about them whenever the opportunity arises. She's also pretty proud of her kinfolk who have made strides in the business, like sister Stella who has achieved a number of chart hits after debuting with *I Want To Hold You In My Dreams Tonight* (1975), and brother Randy who also signed with RCA a couple of years back. There's also another sister, Rachel Dennison, who's been getting herself a name in Hollywood and landed herself Dolly's role in television's 9 To 5 series.

Left: Stella Parton, one of Dolly's sisters, has had several hit records of her own and is now making a name in the theater and on television.

Another RCA artist faring well in country and pop circles is Ronnie Milsap (born Robbinsville, North Carolina, 16 January 1946) who, at the State School for the Blind in Raleigh became interested in classical music but formed a rock group, The Apparitions, because, 'it seemed the thing to do.' More musical crosscutting occurred when he worked with J J Cale and later, in 1965, made his chart debut (on Scepter Records) with a rhythm 'n' blues hit *Never Had It So Good.* He moved into country when he signed a management deal with Jack D Johnson (the svengali behind Charley Pride's early days) and a recording contract with RCA. His first single *I Hate You* (1973) made the Top 10, his third *Pure Love* (1974) was a Number 1. That's the way it's continued, with a dozen, or more, chart toppers including *Legend In My Time* (1974), *Daydreams About Night Things* (1975), *Only One Love In My Life* (1978) and *Why Don't You Spend The Night* (1980) while recent years have seen him building equal success in the pop charts with such as *Smokey Mountain Rain* (1981) and *Any Day Now* (1982). For his success he's received a couple of Grammy Awards and was named CMA Entertainer in 1977.

Milsap's success in the crossover market must be accountable to his background of mixed musical workings and the ease with which he handles a diverse repertoire of material, together with the appeal of his productions handled by Nashville's Tom Collins. This producer has also been responsible for the highly successful recordings of the multitalented Barbara Mandrell, who holds the honor of being the first artist to collect the CMA Entertainer award on two occasions (1980 and 1981), an accolade well befitting her skills as singer, bandleader, multi-instrumentalist and television star. Born

***Left:* Ronnie Milsap started out as a rock singer with his own group, but he gradually moved over to country where he made several top hits.**

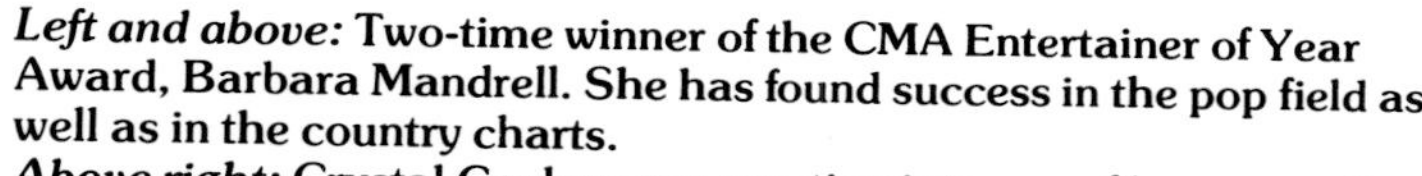

Left and above: **Two-time winner of the CMA Entertainer of Year Award, Barbara Mandrell. She has found success in the pop field as well as in the country charts.**
Above right: **Crystal Gayle pours emotion into one of her romantic songs.**

in Houston, Texas (25 December 1948), she commenced her career young, as a member of the Mandrells family band and, at the age of eleven, was entertaining audiences at the Showboat Hotel, Los Angeles. Two years later, with guest spots on Los Angeles' Town Hall Party television show behind her, she toured with Johnny Cash and, in 1966-67, visited military bases in Korea and Vietnam. Her first records came out on the small Mosrite label but, after a family move to Nashville, she joined Columbia and Billy Sherrill launched her to the country public with covers of pop hits like Otis Redding's *I've Been Loving You Too Long* (1969) and Joe Tex's *Show Me* (1972), though her biggest success was a duet with David Houston, *After Closing Time* (1970). It was the move to ABC/Dot (later to become MCA), and the association with Collins, that took her to the top, beginning with *Standing Room Only* (1975), a ballad that showed off her voice to fine advantage, and followed with songs of a similar styling including *That's What Friends Are For* (1976), *Woman To Woman* (1977) and the Number 1 rating *(If Loving You Is Wrong) I Don't Want To Be Right* (1979), which also put her in the pop charts. In 1982 she firmly captured the spirit of the fans with *I Was Country When Country Wasn't Cool* and, in 1983, went a step further by reaching out to observe the current state of the nation with *In Times Like These,* both showing that she, and her producer, kept their fingers on the pulse of topical events. Barbara Mandrell further delighted the nation's mass audiences by headlining her own NBC-TV series for two seasons, Barbara Mandrell and the Mandrell Sisters, which also spotlighted the talents of sisters Louise, a successful RCA artist with an equally fast-paced stage show, and Irlene, currently carving herself a career in Hollywood as comedienne and actress.

Another talented lady with famed country relations is Crystal Gayle, the younger sister of Loretta Lynn and Peggy Sue and brother of Jay Lee Webb. Born Brenda Gail Webb (Paintsville, Kentucky, 9 January 1951), she worked as a part of her big sister's stage show during her teens and it was Loretta who secured her a deal with Decca, resulting in the chart entry, *I Cried (The Blue Right Out Of My Eyes)* (1970). But it was a switch to United Artists and producer Allen Reynolds that started paying off dividends, with the producer matching her clear voice with smoother sounding, underplayed instrumentation and attractive songs like *Wrong Road Again* (1974), *I'll Get Over You* (1976) and *You Never Miss A Real Good Thing* (1976), which quickly put her at the top of the country charts. Then, with *Don't It Make My Brown Eyes Blue* (1977), she broke over to pop audiences – a situation that continued with *Talkin' In Your Sleep* (1978) and, on Columbia, *Half The Way* (1979). By this time the singer with the waist-length hair had become one of the music's most consistent award winners, with accolades from the CMA, the Academy of Country Music and a Grammy to testify to her considerable success.

In 1982 she made another label move, this time to Elektra, and commenced chart action with *You And I,* a duet performed with Brooklyn-born Eddie Rabbitt (born, 27 November 1947). Of Irish ancestry, he had made his Nashville overtures as a songwriter in the pre-Kristofferson era, scored first success with Roy Drusky *(Working My Way Up From The Bottom)* and moved into the bigtime with hit singles by Elvis Presley (*Kentucky Rain,* 1970) and Ronnie Milsap (*Pure Love,* 1974). By this time he had secured his own recording deal with Elektra and started making chart impact with uptempo, country-founded offerings like *Drinkin' My Baby (Off My Mind)* and *Two Dollars In The Jukebox,* both released in

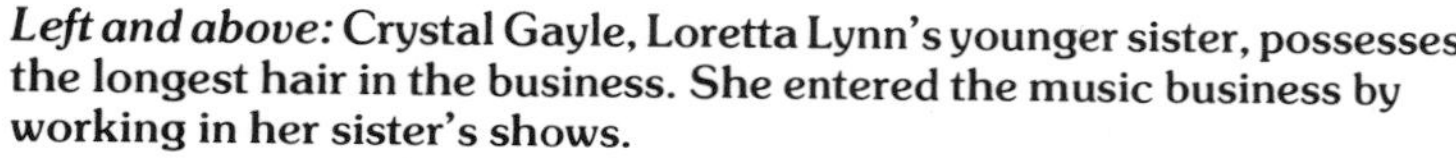

Left and above: **Crystal Gayle, Loretta Lynn's younger sister, possesses the longest hair in the business. She entered the music business by working in her sister's shows.**

Above and next page: **Eddie Rabbitt's Irish origins made the country connection but he has been a crossover artist and a regular pop-chart contender.**

1976, though his styling was to be unpredictable. He moved close to the middle of the road with *I Can't Help Myself* (1977) and *You Don't Love Me Anymore* (1978), and made the pop chart breakthrough with the theme from the Clint Eastwood movie, *Any Which Way But Loose* (1978). He's been a frequent crossover artist ever since, although he may not be all country fans' ideal of a country singer. However, the success of such as *Drivin' My Life Away* (one of the most played records of 1980), *I Love A Rainy Night* (1980), both of which were closer to rockabilly, and *Step By Step* (1981) cannot be ignored.

Mac Davis (born Lubbock, Texas, 21 January 1942) appears to have reversed roles, starting off as a crossover heavy, scoring substantial pop hits with *Baby Don't Get Hooked On Me* (1972) and *Stop And Smell The Roses* (1974), and then moving on to enjoy great success in the country market with the likes of the humorous *It's Hard To Be Humble* (1980) and *Texas In My Rear View Mirror* (1980). He certainly lived the last song, having moved from Texas to Atlanta, Georgia, where he attended Emory University and 'majored in beer with a minor in rock 'n' roll.' He led a rock band and supplemented his income with a variety of jobs including ditch digger, gas station attendant and probation officer, before moving into the record industry as a regional manager for Vee-Jay Records. He was also writing songs and achieved a good break when Lou Rawls cut *You're Good For Me* and came up trumps as Presley took his *In The Ghetto* (1969) to the top of the charts. These days Davis diversifies his activities, with frequent appearances on television. Besides frequent guest slots, he co-hosted the prestigious CMA Awards with Barbara Mandrell in 1981 and 1982, and secured his first starring role in the movies in *North Dallas Forty* (1979).

Perhaps the artist who best reflects the changing face of country is Charlie Daniels (born Wilmington, North Carolina, 28 October 1936) whose music has successfully bridged traditional country music and rock. He explained: 'Nashville is country, but we are not Nashville. We are country, but there's a whole lot more . . .' He illustrated his point with the million-selling *The Devil Went Down To Georgia* (1979) in which Daniels' vocals and fiddle led a frenzied, traditional-styled sound interspersed with rock beats. His roots are right as he's from a background of country and bluegrass, and he's paid his dues (1958-67) playing 'every honky tonk and low life joint from Raleigh to Texas,' performing in a band named The Jaguars. It was on the advice of producer Bob Johnson that he arrived in Nashville and there picked up steady work as a session musician as well as landing his own recording deal on Kama Sutra. At that point the Charlie Daniels Band came into existence and gained initial chart exposure with *Uneasy Rider* (1973) and *The South's Gonna Do It* (1975). A move to Epic eventually brought forth *The Devil* and three CMA Awards in 1979, and the hits kept flowing with the patriotic *In America* (1980) and *Still In Saigon* (1982). Although his music has won the attention of millions of rock fans, the broad, stetson-hatted, tobacco-chewing singer has remained, first and foremost, a loyal supporter of country music and Nashville and, in recent years, has gained a new role as spokesman at numerous conventions and seminars. He also stages his annual Volunteer Jam in Nashville, a lengthy stage concert which features guests from all musical areas.

Undoubtedly the success of the Charlie Daniels Band played a role in getting other Southern country-rock groups like The Marshall Tucker Band, the Allman Brothers and Lynard Skynrd heard within the country marketplace (though chart appearances

Left: Tex-Mex singer Freddy Fender in concert, without his fender guitar.
Below left: Charlie Daniels helped fuse Country and Southern rock music and is one of Nashville's foremost spokesmen.
Below: Mac Davis is a diversified entertainer.

have been virtually nonexistent) and such musicians certainly played a major role in the rejuvenation of Hank Williams Jr's career. But more about that later.

It wasn't just the immediate South that presented a variation of country sounds, nor was country-rock the only variation. Florida, with its easy-listening islands sound, found a hero in Jimmy Buffett who gained an international reputation with such as *Come Monday* (1974) and *Margaritaville* (1977). The same state's Howard and David Bellamy, better known as the Bellamy Brothers, first gained greater pop attention with the chart-topping *Let Your Love Flow* (1976) before moving into stronger country realms with *If I Said You Had A Beautiful Body Would You Hold It Against Me* (1979) and *Sugar Daddy* (1980). More into MOR country-rock was Memphis-based The Amazing Rhythm Aces (featuring Russell Smith, now pursuing a solo career) who captured a lot of country attention with *Third Rate Romance* (1975) and *Amazing Grace (Used To Be Her Favorite Song)* (1975), and the outrageous Dr. Hook. They featured eye-patched Ray Sawyer and vocalist Dennis Locorrier and based themselves in Nashville after a much talked-about appearance on the Grand Ole Opry. The group scored with such as *If Not You* (1976) and *When You're In Love With A Beautiful Woman* (1979).

Then, from Colorado by way of California, came the Nitty Gritty Dirt Band (more simply known as the Dirt Band these days) who first scored success with *Some Of Shelly's Blues* (1969) and *Mr. Bojangles* (1970). In 1973 the group – then featuring Jimmie Fadden, Jeff Hanna, Jim Ibbotson, John McEuan and Les Thompson – came up with a project that not only brought traditional country to the ears of the rock market but also won the overall praise of the country industry. It was named *Will The Circle Be Unbroken,* an ambitious three-album set that combined the group with many of country's historical figures including Roy Acuff, Mother Maybelle Carter, Earl Scruggs, Merle Travis and Doc Watson. The results proved that long-haired musicians and traditional performers could blend perfectly to produce a masterpiece. The sounds of the albums were far superior to the major label

Left: **In the 1965 era ex-Cricket Waylon Jennings' image was more clean cut than his outlaw image of a decade later.**

Nashville productions, supposedly the foundation of country music.

Another hybrid sound arose from the Texas-Mexican border and was known simply as Tex-Mex. Baldemar Huerta – more familiarly known as Freddy Fender (born San Benito, Texas, 4 June 1937) – was a veteran performer who had spent twenty years working beer joints and Chicano dance halls, cutting Spanish records and had served a stretch for possession of grass. In 1975 he brought Tex-Mex into the limelight and rose to the top of the charts with the million-selling *Before The Next Teardrop Falls,* produced by another veteran of the industry, Huey Meaux. A second million seller quickly followed, a revival of his earlier *Wasted Days And Wasted Nights* (1975), and although hits continued with *Secret Love* (1975) and *You'll Lose A Real Good Thing* (1976), the novelty of Fender's English-Spanish presentations had worn a little thin by the end of the decade. Far more successful, on a long-term basis, has been Johnny Rodriguez (born Sabinal, Texas, 10 December 1952) who, after brushing with the law following the kidnapping and barbecuing of a goat, started entertaining tourists at Happy Shahan's famed Alamo Village in Bracketville, Texas. There he was 'discovered' by Bobby Bare and Tom T. Hall, who encouraged him to come to Nashville. He joined Hall's Storytellers band and signed with Mercury. His single, *Pass Me By* (1972) made the Top 10 and from there it was only a short distance to the Number 1 slot, which he hit three times during the next 12 months with *You Always Come Back (To Hurting Me), Ridin' My Thumb To Mexico* and *That's The Way Love Goes.* He made another two-dozen chart appearances before the decade was out and then, signing with Epic and Sherrill, continued on top with such as *How Could I Love Her So Much* (1983).

Other Texas musicians blended the Lone Star State's traditional honky-tonk sound and western swing with rock, contemporary country and other influences. Joe Ely, from Lubbock, first worked in country as a member of the short-lived Flatlanders (which also featured other cult singer/songwriters Butch Hancock and Jimmie Dale Gilmore) and received considerable praise for his early MCA albums, though his later recordings moved into a rockabilly vein. A one-time member of the Ely band was steel-guitarist Lloyd Maines who, after independently recording four albums as a member of the Maines Brothers, secured a major label deal with Mercury in 1983. These artists built up enthusiastic followings in Austin, the state's capital and the center of a new, innovative country movement that was entirely distinct from the sounds generated in other locations. It bred such talent as Marcia Ball, who achieved a minor chart success with *I'm A Fool To Care* (1977), as well as making local waves under the name of Freida and the Firedogs; western-swing bands like Asleep At The Wheel and Alvin Crow and the Pleasant Valley Boys; and the notorious 'Kinky' Friedman, known as the 'Texas Jewboy' and establishing a reputation as the Frank Zappa of country music, whose bitter-sweet lyrics achieved a national hit in *Sold American* (1973).

Others arrived in Austin, finding that the city – with its mixed cultural influences and enthusiastic audiences, comprising both old-timers and students – was an ideal creative environment. Jerry Jeff Walker, one of Austin's most colorful characters, came from New York and first formed a rock band, Circus Maximus, before gaining a reputation as a progressive singer/songwriter. Among his many original songs were *Mr. Bojangles* and *Railroad Lady* (which he co-wrote with Jimmy Buffett, and provided a 1974 hit for Lefty Frizzell) while presenting a regular output of albums on MCA. Michael Murphey, like Walker, was a one-time member of the urban folk scene and developed a part-hippie, part-redneck 'cosmic cowboy' image. He gained a vast following with songs like *Geronimo's Cadillac* (1972), *Carolina In The Pines* (1975) and *Renegade* (1976), all of which displayed his loving interest in western heritage and its changing face. More recently, Murphey shot back into the high chart regions, albeit with a crossover styling, with *What's Forever For* (1982). Guy Clark also spent time in Austin (as well as Los Angeles and Nashville). He is a singer/songwriter who has given country some of its most poetic lyrics in *Desperados Waiting For A Train, L.A. Freeway* and *The Last Gunfighter Ballad,* as well as whipping up acclaim for his debut album *Old No. 1* (1975) though, as yet, hasn't broken into the recording bigtime. Showing that Austin's reputation stretches far and wide, London's Wes McGhee has been making the city a frequent stopping-off place for his recordings, using local musicians and impressing all and sundry with his own distinctive songs.

It was this environment, and the complete freedom of artistic expression, that attracted Willie Nelson to Austin, quickly to

Left: **'My heroes have always been cowboys and they still are it seems/ Sadly in search of, and one step in back of, themselves and their slow-moving dreams! . . .' go the words to Waylon Jennings 1970s hit.**
Right: **After 20 years of struggle, Willie Nelson was presenting his music his own way, gaining movie stardom as well.**

become city hero and father figure to all other musicians, singers and songwriters.

In 1976 RCA released a compilation album that was to make country-music history by selling well over one million copies. The title was *Wanted: The Outlaws,* the brainchild of the label's Jerry Bradley, and featured music by Waylon Jennings, Willie Nelson, Jessi Colter and Tompall Glaser, all artists who weren't interested in the Nashville way of doing things or bastardizing their music in order to succeed in the crossover market. They were, purely and simply, interested in performing *their* music *their* way and, through the years of battling with the establishment, had become labeled the 'Nashville Rebels.' The overall result, besides achieving amazing sales, brought the music to the attention of pop and rock audiences and established a new word (albeit shortlived) into musical dictionaries, 'outlaw' – a term that Jennings abhored and said as much in his song *Don't You Think This Outlaw Bit's Done Got Out Of Hand* (1978).

The success of the album for Waylon Jennings (born Littlefield, Texas, 15 June 1937) meant the ultimate breakthrough for a career that was reaching fruition a couple of years earlier with the top hits *This Time* and *I'm A Ramblin' Man* (1974). A former deejay, he made his radio debut on a hometown radio station at the age of twelve and, in 1958, moved to Lubbock where he met up with Buddy Holly and was hired as his group's bass player. (It was Jennings who gave up his seat to J P Richardson, 'The Big Bopper,' on that fateful plane flight, another subject that the singer feels has 'got out of hand.') In the early 1960s he settled in Phoenix, Arizona, formed the Waylors and began gigging at the city's JD's Club, building a reputation that would eventually reach the ears of Chet Atkins. His first RCA singles were promoted as the more folksy side of the Nashville Sound, and scored chart successes with such as *(That's What You Get) For Loving Me* (1966), *Walk On Out Of My Mind* (1968) and *Only Daddy That'll Walk The Line* (1968). He also appeared in the movie *Nashville Rebel* (1966), a title that was equally applicable to the singer's own real-life personna as, by the beginning of the 1970s, he was bucking the system by using material from the new writers in town as well as making producer and musician demands – and, when Nashville objected, Jennings went over its head and straight to RCA's head office in New York. He won out, gaining for himself an independent production deal in which he presented the recordings to the label for releasing.

His endeavors began reaping rewards as he cut material from writers such as Kristofferson, Steve Young, Lee Clayton and Billy Joe Shaver, resulting in innovative albums like *Ladies Love Outlaws* (1972), *Lonesome, On'ry And Mean* (1973) and *Honky Tonk Heroes* (1973) while paying tribute to his heritage, his own way, with the double-sided, Number 1 hit single *Are You Sure Hank Done It This Way* coupled with *Bob Wills Is Still The King* (1975). After proving that he could, very successfully, do it his way, *Wanted: The Outlaws* brought Jennings to the attention of a mass record-buying public. As an additional bonus, it whipped up acclaim for his duet work with close-friend and occasional recording-partner Willie Nelson. Jennings and Nelson were first heard together by the country scene on the chart-topping *Good Hearted Woman* (1975) and, a couple of years later, joined forces on the equally memorable album *Waylon & Willie.* From there on it was success all the way for Jennings as the top singles mounted up with *Luckenbach, Texas (Back To The Basics Of Life)* (1977), *I've Always Been Crazy* (1978), *Amanda* (1979) and *Good Ol' Boys* (1980), the million-selling theme from television's Dukes Of Hazzard.

Willie Nelson (born Abbott, Texas, 30 April 1933) had been a victim of the Nashville system for even longer and, like Jennings, had started off in radio, doubling as announcer and musician on a Fort Worth station in the mid-1950s while pursuing his songwriting ambitions (*Family Bible* was written around this time). His first breaks came while playing bass in Ray Price's band, with cuts coming from such as Patsy Cline (*Crazy*, 1961), Faron Young (*Hello Walls*, 1961) and Price (*Night Life*, 1963) and the writer's own minor label efforts getting him major breaks on, first, Liberty and, in 1965, RCA. But he fitted uncomfortably into Nashville's way of doing things, his scat, jazz-styled vocals mustered little enthusiasm from the almost-closeted world of 1960s country and, out of seventeen chart singles released during the period 1962-71, only one made the Top 20 *(Bring Me Sunshine*, 1968). He became disillusioned and the burning down of his Nashville home gave him the final reason for quitting town. He headed back to Texas and found a new base in Austin where, besides representing a figure of experience to the city's young musicians, he adopted a drastic change of image. Suddenly the clean-cut struggling Nashville recording artist became the Austin hippie, with the familiar long hair, beard, tee shirt and jeans. He signed a new deal with Atlantic, produced two highly praised, personalized albums – *Shotgun Willie* (1973) and *Phases And Stages* (1974) – and confirmed his standing as the consolidating figure in the new Texas movement

***Left and above:* 'Cowboys like smokey old pool rooms and clear mountain mornings/Lone Star belt buckles and old faded Levis . . .' Willie Nelson spent many years striving for Nashville recognition before becoming a father figure of the 'outlaws' movement.**
***Above left:* It is essentially autobiographical when Waylon Jennings sings 'I grew up a dreamin' of being a cowboy and loving the cowboy ways/pursuing the life of my high-riding heroes I burned up my childhood days . . .'**

with the staging of his annual Dripping Springs festivals. The first was held on 4 July 1972, and traditional acts like Roy Acuff and Tex Ritter performed alongside their contemporary compatriots.

The Atlantic deal, and the label's commitment to country, was shortlived and Nelson moved on to Columbia. His opening gambit was the self-produced concept album *Red Headed Stranger* (1975), a best seller in both country and rock circles and the outlet for the million-selling single *Blue Eyes Crying In The Rain.* By the time of the *Outlaws* arrival Nelson's success was assured; from then on he merely built upon it by continuing with recordings that remained nonconforming and unpredictable, one moment cutting a 'down to the roots' tribute album to Lefty Frizzell, and the next working with Leon Russell and cutting a live concert set with his equally unorthordox Family band. His biggest success came in 1978 with *Stardust*, an album of pop standards produced and arranged by Booker T Jones which, six years later, was still in the charts with over three-million sales to its credit. Such success has ensured that virtually all his past recordings have resurfaced, while his new output has included duet offerings with Webb Pierce, Ray Price and, recently, the award-winning set with Merle Haggard, *Poncho And Lefty* (1983). With the 1979 CMA Entertainer trophy secured, he commenced an equally successful career as a movie star.

The other members of the *Outlaws* quartet didn't fare nearly as well, although Waylon's wife, Jessi Colter, had secured a million seller with *I'm Not Lisa* (1975), a song that she 'wrote in five minutes,' several months before the album came out. Formerly married to guitarist Duane Eddy (she performed in this roadshow on several overseas tours), this singer/songwriter has also secured other hit singles including *Whatever Happened to Blue Eyes* (1975) and *It's Morning* (1976) as well as recording a number of albums which show off her writing skills and very distinctive styling. Currently this much underrated performer appears on the road with her husband.

The 'outlaw' tag well suited Tompall Glaser (born Spaulding, Nebraska, 3 September 1933) for he, along with his younger brothers Chuck (born 27 February 1936) and Jim (born 16 December 1937), was running things his own way before such activities became fashionable. As a vocal trio, they arrived in Nashville in 1958 after success on Arthur Godfrey Talent Scouts and soon found a niche in the town's blossoming recording scene – they provided harmonies on Marty Robbins' *El Paso* among other recordings – as well as securing their own deal on Decca, though here they were projected as a folk act. Once signed to MGM, they quickly fitted into the country mainstream with smooth offerings like *Through The Eyes Of Love* (1967), *California Girl* (1969) and *Rings* (1971) and were named Vocal Group Of The Decade by the trade publication Record World. At the same they started building their own industrial empire (virtually unheard of at the time), comprising recording, production and publishing concerns, and quickly became a focal point and haven for the gathering 'new breed' of songwriters. Undoubtedly this fresh talent was the catalyst for Tompall Glaser to start presenting his own individual ideas, and the brothers split to go their own artistic ways in 1973.

His first solo offering arrived on MGM – the well-received *Charlie* (1973) album – while a change of labels to ABC, and the formation of his Outlaws band, saw him adopting a much heavier, funkier approach to his music which suited his gruff voice though did not endear itself too well to the public. The outcome was a number of innovative albums but only one Top 50 single, *It'll Be Her* (1977) resulting, finally, in the brothers getting back together again to

HONEYSUCKLE
ROSE

Previous page and below: Willie Nelson performing alone and with his family in London for a 1982 concert visit. His wife, Jessi Colter, has several hits in her own right.

Right: **Larry Gatlin, one of Nashville's most creative songwriters, blends outstanding close harmonies with his brothers Steve and Rudy.**

record a top single with Kristofferson's *Loving Her Was Easier* (1981). The 'togetherness' did not last long this time around and, in 1983, Jim Glaser made the split to pursue a solo career on the strength of a number of chart singles.

Another singer/songwriter fitting the outlaw mold was David Allan Coe (born Akron, Ohio, 6 September 1939), whose arrival in Nashville in 1967 followed some twenty years in reform schools, institutions and prisons (including, although disputed by some sources, a stretch on Death Row at the Ohio State Penitentiary for killing an inmate). He launched his career on Shelby Singleton's SSS label with blues recordings and moved into country under the guise of 'The Mysterious Rhinestone Cowboy,' which saw him making stage appearances in black rhinestone costume and mask, and traveling around in a long black hearse. His early years with Columbia provided only minimal success in singles terms, but his albums – which, frequently, told a continuing biographical tale – have all sold well, no doubt gaining momentum when linked to his notorious lifestyle that included living with several wives (according to his Mormon faith) and association with motor-cycle gangs. Initially his greatest successes came as a songwriter, having collected monster hits in *Would You Lay With Me In A Field Of Stone* (Tanya Tucker, 1974) and *Take This Job And Shove It* (Johnny Paycheck, 1977) as well as scoring modest success for himself with *Waylon, Willie And Me* (1976). In 1983 his chart activities really took off as he went to the top with *The Ride*, the tale of a ghostly meeting with Hank Williams.

The 1970s saw the greatest emergence of artists in the music's history and, as the crossover market grew and the media became ever more willing to focus its attention on country talent, so the doorways opened even wider. An artist who masterfully weaved together the roles of songwriter and singer is Larry Gatlin (born Seminole, Texas, 2 May 1948). Possessing gospel roots, he originally formed a gospel group with his younger brothers Steve and Rudy. He originally intended to pursue a career in law, but music won out and he became a member of The Imperials gospel quartet. It was through Dottie West's encouragement, and her recording of several of his songs, that he arrived in Nashville and there found influential support in Johnny Cash and Kris Kristofferson – the first using several of his songs in the *Gospel Road* movie and the latter opening up the doorways to a Monument recording deal, resulting in the debut album *The Pilgrim* (1974). His reputation was established with *Broken Lady* (1975) and *Statues Without Hearts* (1976), and he first made the top of the charts with *I Just Wish You Were Someone I Love* (1977). Since then he's kept the hits flowing with songs like *All The Gold In California* (1979), *Take Me To Your Loving Place* (1980) and *Sure Feels Like Love* (1982), all displaying his fine intricate lyrics, born out of 'a love affair with the English language' during his University of Houston days, and rounded to perfection with the close harmonies of his younger brothers. Today all three Gatlins are an integral part of a musical unit that also includes musicians, though Larry still gets the star billing.

Several artists emerged from rock sources, like North Carolina's Billy 'Crash' Craddock who originally scored with the pop song *Don't Deliver Me* (1959) and made a successful career out of country a couple of decades later. He made more than 30 chart appearances in the 1970s, kicking off with *Knock Three Times* (1971) and crossed over twice in 1974 with *Rub It In* and *Ruby Baby*. Craddock is also one of country's most energetic stage performers. Another one-time rocker, Freddy Weller (from Atlanta,

Georgia), once worked with Paul Revere and the Raiders before putting the pop scene behind him, although continuing to draw upon it for his greatest hits like *Games People Play* (1969) and *Promised Land* (1970). Billy Swan, who's equally at ease with both country and rock, first gained fame as the writer of Clyde McPhatter's *Lover Please* (1962) and then topped the country and pop charts with his multimillion-selling *I Can Help* (1974). He also handles record production and, whenever the occasion arises, takes to the road as a member of Kris Kristofferson's band. Possessing an even wider musical career, Oklahoma-born Hoyt Axton (who's mother, Nashville-publicist Mae Boren Axton, penned Presley's *Heartbreak Hotel*), first recorded in a folk vein and wrote hits for pop groups like Steppenwolf *(The Pusher)* and Three Dog Night *(Never Been To Spain)* before scoring a massive international country hit with *Della And The Dealer* (1979), released on his own Jeremiah label. Besides many albums to his credit, Axton has also built up a successful acting career with television guest appearances on McCloud and Bionic Woman and a starring role in the movie *The Black Stallion* (1979).

Artists such as Danny Davis and the Nashville Brass and Dave & Sugar brought more innovations to country. Davis, a former big-band sideman and Connie Francis' hit-record producer, first conceived the idea of adding brass to a country rhythm section while working as a production assistant to Chet Atkins. The idea materialized as The Nashville Brass and, although the group remained a steady album seller and stage attraction, hardly amounted to anything in the singles charts. Far more successful were Dave & Sugar, a trio originally put together by Dave Rowland – a one-time member of Presley's touring group The Stamps Quartet – as backup singers for Charley Pride, but developed into a strong harmony group in their own right. Besides Rowland, the trio's original lineup also featured Jackie Franz and Vicki Hackman and they hit success with their second single, *The Door Is Always Open* (1976), topping the charts. Besides scoring more than a dozen hits during the decade – including *Tear Time* (1978) and *Golden Tears* (1979) – their close, almost pop-styled harmonies were accompanied by slick stage work, but their eventual demise is probably attributable to too many personnel changes. A later member was Sue Powell, currently seeking out a solo career with a couple of chart singles on RCA behind her. The Kendalls, who originally hailed from St Louis, Missouri, provided the rather unique teaming of father and daughter, Royce and Jeannie. They first arrived in Nashville during the late 1960s to make some custom recordings, but the results were impressive enough for Stop Records to sign the duo, resulting in their first chart entry, *Leavin' On A Jet Plane* (1970). It was seven years later, though, that they really hit the bigtime with *Heaven's Just A Sin Away*, a song that was recorded as an afterthought (and only released through deejay enthusiasm). It went to the top of the charts and collected both CMA and Grammy Awards. Subsequently, they've maintained their success with regular chart appearances including another Number 1 in *Sweet Desire/Old Fashioned Love* (1978).

The decade was also very good for the ladies in country music, although none managed to equal the success of Debbie Boone

From left to right: **Royce and Jeannie Kendall, the father and daughter team; Johnny Rodriquez, singer of the Tex-Mex sound; Gene Watson, professional from the age of 13; and Billie Jo Spears, a chart artist in both the US and Britain.**

(daughter of 1950s' pop-idol, Pat) who – after gaining experience singing with her sisters and mother as The Boone Girls – branched out on a solo career. In 1977 she hit the top of a variety of charts with *You Light Up My Life*, which quickly became one of the best-selling singles of all time. She then moved into the country market with a number of chart records, including another Number 1 with *Are You On The Road To Lovin' Me Again* (1980).

Although no others could equal the initial Boone success, women did score well in crossover terms, with North Carolina's Donna Fargo – after teaching school in California while struggling to get her music across on a succession of small labels – hitting the heights of the country and pop charts via the Dot label. This distinctive, dry-throated stylist broke through with her original song *Happiest Girl In The Whole USA* (1972), a million seller which was immediately followed by another Gold Disc victor, *Funny Face*. In their wake came a couple of dozen more chart entries during the decade – including *Superman* (1973) and *That Was Yesterday* (1977) – while, on stage, she presented slick, Las Vegas-styled performances.

Barbara Fairchild, another singer with a very distinctive voice and humorous personality, was brought to Columbia by Billy Sherrill, though it was Jan Crutchfield who produced her crossover hit *Teddy Bear Song* (1972). She continued with songs such as *Kid Stuff* (1973) and *Baby Doll* (1974), but the successes grew less as the years passed and sadly, by the early 1980s, she had disappeared from Nashville's recording scene. Mega's Marilyn Sellers had an even shorter career, just four hits in a two-year period – one of them was the substantial country-pop success *One Day At A Time* (1974), penned by Marijohn Wilkin and Kris Kristofferson. Jeanne Pruett, who arrived in Nashville in 1958, was writing her own songs and looking after her family while husband Jack played guitar in the Marty Robbins band. Eventually she started recording herself, with *Satin Sheets* (1973) – not one of her originals, this written by John Volinkaty – turning out the most successful of her twenty or so hits. These days she's one of the popular attractions on the Grand Ole Opry.

Texas-born Billie Jo Spears was first heard on record at the tender age of thirteen with *Too Old For Toys, Too Young For Boys*, though she didn't start scoring chart success until an association with Capitol and *Mr. Walker It's All Over* (1969). A move to United Artists made her an even bigger star with the Number 1 *Blanket On The Ground* (1975), and she kept star status with other attractive offerings, including *What I've Got In Mind* (1976) and *'57 Chevrolet* (1978). After a slight lapse in releases, she returned to the charts in 1984 with *Midnight Blue* on the new independent Parliament label. Her bluesy voice and downhome personality has also brought her success overseas, particularly in Britain where she's had several pop chart successes and enjoys regular sell-out concert tours. Another long-time favorite, Melba Montgomery, must have surprised a lot of people when her rich Alabama voice

Above: Donna Fargo made the charts in 1972 with *Happiest Girl in the Whole USA*, which was followed by many more.
Left: Billie Jo Spears is the most successful of Nashville's country singers on the British pop charts.
Top: Jeanne Pruett is the songwriter who rose to success with *Satin Sheets* in 1973 and remains a country favorite.
Next page: The group Asleep at the Wheel started out in San Francisco and moved to Austin, Texas in the 1970s.

WHN

Above: Keeping the sound of real country music alive during the age of crossovers, Moe Bandy says he couldn't sing it any other way.
Above left: Another successful singer of the 1970s with titles like _Gwen_ (1971) and _Heaven is My Woman's Love_ (1972), Tommy Overstreet presented an easy listening feel to country music.
Left: The Bellamy Brothers, Howard and David, brought the sound of Florida to country music during the 1970s.
Right: British-born singer Olivia Newton-John was a center of controversy after winning one of country music's top awards in the 1970s.
Below left: Billie Swann, creator of the hit song _I Can Help_ which made him famous, is seen on the road regularly with Kris Kristofferson.

(which makes her one of the most country of all country singers) was heard in the pop charts with *No Charge* (1974), a semi-narration that tugged at the heartstrings of sentimentalists. Among her earlier successes was the classic duet with George Jones, *We Must Have Been Out Of Our Minds* (1963).

Then there were those male singers who couldn't sing it any other way but country, like Oklahoma's Cal Smith who, after making chart appearances for several years, went straight to the top in 1974 with *Country Bumpkin* and *It's Time To Pay The Fiddler*. But the first of the singers to present a 1970s revival of solid honky-tonk traditions was Moe Bandy (born Meridian, Mississippi, 12 February 1944), who was raised to the sound of his parents' own musical skills and Jimmie Rodgers' and Hank Williams' recordings. A one-time broncbuster who decided that singing was a safer occupation, he first gained national recognition when his self-financed *I Just Started Hatin' Cheatin' Songs Today* (1974)

Left and right: Kenny Rogers and Dottie West, his regular singing partner, on stage and in the recording studio.

was released on the short-lived GRC label. Less than two years later, he was on Columbia and right at the top with *Hank Williams You Wrote My Life* (1975), a song that suited his voice and image to perfection. 'Nobody can ever change me, and I don't believe they ever will because I'm too solidly country,' he once remarked – and nobody would ever want to as his output of traditional-styled, barroom hoppin' and slippin' around songs have always kept the public aware of what honest-to-goodness country music is all about. With spirited production by Ray Baker, he's kept the output steady with releases such as *Soft Lights And Country Music* (1978) and *I Cheated Me Right Out Of You* (1979) and launched into an equally successful duet partnership with Joe Stampley (a former member of the 1960s pop group The Uniques, before he hit the country heights with *Soul Song* in 1972) on *Just Good Ol' Boys* (1979). The charms of Judy Bailey and Becky Hobbs also joined Bandy on *Following The Feeling* (1980) and *Let's Get Over Them Together* (1983) respectively.

Gene Watson (born Palestine, Texas, 11 October 1943) won out with the country fans on *Love In The Hot Afternoon* (1975) after having begun his professional career at the age of thirteen on radio and notching up many local hits in the Houston area. A singer with an easy-flowing style and a powerful voice, his subsequent successes – which included *Paper Rosie* (1977), *Cowboys Don't Get Lucky All The Time* (1978) and *Farewell Party* (1979) – made him one of Capitol's major country sellers and living proof that there was still a place for real country in spite of heated crossover activities. In 1981 he moved over to the MCA roster and maintained the hit flow with *This Dream's On Me* (1982) and *Sometimes I Get Lucky And Forget* (1983).

The western image also flourished, partly owing to the 'outlaws' movement and partly to the presence of singers like Ed Bruce (born Keiser, Arkansas), who presented a genuinely rugged, outdoor appearance. Although he started his recording career in Memphis on Sun, at that time he spent the greater part of his time working on his father's used-automobile lot, and it wasn't until he made the move to Nashville in the mid-1960s that he started pursuing country ambitions in earnest. He achieved a few minor hits on RCA and Monument, but first achieved success as his rich voice and fine writing skills combined on the contemporary classic *Mamas, Don't Let Your Babies Grow Up To Be Cowboys* (1975) on United Artists and further developed the image with *When I Die Just Let Me Go To Texas* (1977). A move to MCA brought further successes with songs such as *Diane* (1980) and *The Last Cowboy Song* (1980), a splendidly poignant seminarration which also featured the voice of Willie Nelson. As his success grew, Bruce, guided by his manager and wife Patsy, broke into television and secured a starring role in the series Brett Maverick (1981/82) as well as being featured in many advertisements including the State of Tennessee and Big Duke Chewing Tobacco.

By the decade's end there was little doubt as to who was the biggest star of the 1970s. The name, of course, was Kenny Rogers, a singer who made crossover an everyday occurrence and whose grainy voice attracted all manner of listeners and whose recordings made the top of most charts, irrespective of categorizations. A singer with a country-music background, Rogers (born Houston, Texas, 21 August 1938) worked his way through 'six different phases of music' before getting back to the sounds of his roots in the mid-1970s. He made his first recording while still in high school, obtaining a local hit with *Crazy Feeling* (1958), and started attracting national attention as he played avant-garde jazz with the Bobby Doyle Trio and popular folk as a 'third generation' member of the New Christy Minstrals. Then, on 10 July 1967, he and three other Minstrals announced the creation of The First Edition and, within six months, were climbing up the pop charts with *Just Dropped In (To See What Condition My Condition Was In)*. Although basically a pop-folk-rock group, their other big seller was a country song, Mel Tillis' *Rudy, Don't Take Your Love To Town* (1969).

In the mid-1970s, with the First Edition behind him, Rogers arrived in Nashville to seek out songs. He had signed with United Artists and was set to work with producer Larry Butler who promised that, 'working the right plan of campaign, he would make a successful country and pop singer out of me within a year,' recalls the singer. Butler was just about right. A little more than twelve months after his first release, *Love Lifted Me* (1975), the multi-million selling *Lucille* (1977) – a pure country song – took him right to the top of both charts as well as reaching out into many international markets. A few months later he was back with another million seller, *Daytime Friends*, this time the presentation was a little less country, a little more uptempo pop. By the 1980s he had another six Number 1s under his belt, none of which maintained a predictable format as he switched from hard country – *The Gambler* (1978), the award-winning song written by Don Schlitz,

Above: **Dottie West in front of her tour bus.**
Right: **Kenny Rogers was a 1960s pop star who became a 1970s country sensation and then a 1980s international superstar.**

and *Coward Of The County* (1979) – to the plaintive balladry of *You Decorated My Life* (1979) and *Lady* (1980). He also found an ideal stage and recording partner in stalwart Dottie West (who, incidentally, had started her own chart career with *Love Is No Excuse*, a duet with Jim Reeves in 1964). Together they reaped success with *All I Ever Needed Is You* (1979) and *'Til I Can Make It On My Own* (1979) and, in 1980, he joined forces with Kim Carnes on *Don't Fall In Love With A Dreamer*, culled from the highly acclaimed concept-album *Gideon*.

A great deal of Kenny Rogers' success must be accountable to his shrewd business sense and working knowledge of the music industry (explained in his 1978 book *Making It In Music*), but with the acumen of his manager, Ken Kragen, became one of the world's most highly paid entertainers. An SRO box office attraction, he guested on all the top television shows (and, sometimes, hosted them himself) and was rewarded with Grammies and other awards from such bodies as the Country Music Association and the Academy of Country Music as well as collecting numerous trade accolades. On the recording front he moved more into a MOR format as he worked with producer Lionel Richie (of the Commodores) on *Share Your Love With Me* (1981), *Through The Years* (1982) and *We've Got Tonight* (1983), the last being a duet with Scotland's pop superstar, Sheena Easton. In late 1983, following one of the most lucrative deals ever made in recording history, he debuted on RCA – and what better way than to commence the association than with that label's own phenomenal talent, Dolly Parton. The result was another multimillion selling single, *Islands In The Sun*. Rogers' success didn't stop there though. Like so many other star names in recent years, he found a readymade niche in the movies.

The New Dimensions of Country

As country music gained greater and greater popularity, and its appeal reached mass-audience attention, it was only natural that television and the movies should sit up and take notice – and react. By the early 1980s the appearances of country artists within these mediums became almost commonplace and, as Hollywood and television sought out every conceivable situation in which to use a country star, the spinoffs in advertising and records created an even larger snowball.

On television, during the period September 1981 to August 1982, country music was featured in more than two dozen 'specials' on American networks, attracting an average of 30 percent of the population, and hardly ever less than 25 percent. Among the artists featured were Loretta Lynn, Johnny Cash, John Denver, Barbara Mandrell, Anne Murray and Hoyt Axton, with even veteran Roy Acuff getting his own NBC special in celebration of '50 Years The King of Country Music.' When movies like Clint Eastwood's *Every Which Way But Loose* and Kenny Rogers' *The Coward Of The Country* were screened by CBS, they virtually wiped out all viewing competition.

Of course, television had featured country music in small degrees since the early 1950s, with Gene Autry taking the singing cowboy to the small screen on his own CBS series (1950-56) and the West Coast's Town Hall Party sustaining a ten-year run commencing in 1951. Eddy Arnold was among the first to host a network show, stepping in as Perry Como's summer replacement on NBC in 1952, and four years later getting his own show that originated from Springfield, Missouri. Among the other artists to secure a show on the strength of hit record success were George Hamilton IV, who hosted a lunchtime show on ABC in 1959, and Roger Miller on NBC during the period 1966-67.

However, the syndication market provided far greater opportunities. Among the most successful of these shows was Porter Wagoner's, which commenced its long run in 1960 with eighteen stations' support but, by the decade's end, had increased to over 100 throughout the States and Canada. Bill Anderson had a series of 39 shows in 1966, seen in 126 cities, but by the late 1970s had developed into a substantial television personality as he hosted the game show, The Better Sex, made appearances on the daytime soap opera One Life To Live and introduced the syndicated Backstage At The Grand Ole Opry.

More stars were to be seen on the television variations of popular radio shows, like Springfield's Ozark Jubilee hosted by Red Foley during the 1950s on NBC, and the monthly Grand Ole Opry shows screened by ABC. In 1966 the Opry reappeared again, this time under the auspices of 39 syndicated half-hour shows. The music also added to the rural flavoring of a trio of the 1960s top-rating situation comedies – The Beverly Hillbillies (which provided an international hit for Lester Flatt and Earl Scruggs in its theme tune), Petticoat Junction and Green Acres.

The singer who played a pioneering role in bringing country to the television screens was Jimmy Dean (born Plainview, Texas, 10 August 1928) who started out by playing a variety of instuments at the age of ten. While in the Air Force he joined other servicemen in the group The Tennessee Haymakers, playing dates in their off-duty hours around Washington, DC, and he remained in the area after his discharge. In 1953, on the strength of his local popularity and a national hit *(Bummin' Around),* he gained his first television show. Then, during the 1950s, Dean hosted weekday and Saturday-evening shows on WMAL-TV until his popularity had grown so much that he gained a network show on CBS. His big break came on the heels of his big sellers *Big Bad John* (1961), *P.T. 109* (1962) and *Little Black Book* (1962) when, based in New York, he was rewarded by ABC with a top-line variety show (1963-66) which, during its run, was given prime-time viewing. Although in recent years he's concentrated more on his sausage business, he made a brief comeback with the million-selling narration *I.O.U.* (1976) and has been seen regularly on syndication, his latest series being Jimmy Dean's Country Beat, launched during January 1984 and featuring many top-line country artists as guests.

The Dean shows, together with country artists' appearances on top chat programs like The Mike Douglas Show, set the pace and in 1969 both Johnny Cash and Glen Campbell were given prime time series by ABC and CBS respectively, though the latter's Goodtime

Right: **Barbara Mandrell had her own show on television for two years running.**

Above: **Homer and Jethro combined comedy with country music.**
Top: **Flatt and Scruggs, famous fiddle and banjo duo, did the theme music for the Beverly Hillbillies television show.**
Right: **Sissy Spacek won an Oscar for her role as Loretta Lynn in *Coal Miner's Daughter*.**

Hour provided guests from wider spheres than just country. A third series, Hee Haw (CBS), didn't try to hide away any country origins and, with Buck Owens and Roy Clark leading the proceedings (with good support from such as Grandpa Jones, Archie Campbell and Lulu Roman), it could be best described as a hillbilly 'laugh-in,' complete with colorful characters, hick comedy and country music. All three shows were relatively shortlived though and, in 1971, CBS decided to axe any show with a rural flavoring, including the popular sitcoms headed up by The Beverly Hillbillies. Nevertheless Hee Haw survived, with producer Sam Lovullo promptly putting it into syndication, where it has kept loyal public support up to the present time.

The 1970s were pretty lean years for country on the networks, although the awards presentations of the Country Music Association and the Academy of Country Music became regular fare. However, where the majors feared to tread, the Public Broadcast System (PBS) found a surefire winner in Austin City Limits, carried on 90 percent of the network's stations. (This show piloted in 1974 with Willie Nelson, and the artist returned seven years later to present his complete *Over The Rainbow* album as a 'special.') PBS has also transmitted presentations of the Grand Ole Opry, and its Soundstage program maintained a healthy proportion of country and folk acts as well as the usual presentations of rock and popular music.

Country found a ready market in syndication, with Nashville's Show Biz Inc, one of the most active producers of programs. In its early days the company was responsible for shows such as The Porter Wagoner Show, The Wilburn Brothers Show and Country Crossroads (headlined by Del Reeves and Jamey Ryan) while, more recently, the long-running Pop Goes The Country, Backstage At The Grand Ole Opry and The Best Of Porter And Dolly. (Dolly Parton was also seen in her own series in 1976, Dolly, which on one memorable occasion also featured the talents of Linda Ronstadt and Emmylou Harris.) A major source for syndicated 'specials' is Jim Owens Productions which, besides presenting the fan-orientated Music City News Awards, also produced shows on Chet Atkins, Jerry Reed, Barbi Benton and a tribute to Hank Williams, one of country music's best loved and most respected stars.

By the 1980s, as country had weaved itself into the entertainment mainstream, the networks reversed previous decisions and once again started bringing the music back into their schedules, this time in the form of 'specials' although Barbara Mandrell was the only entertainer to gain a series. Titled Barbara Mandrell and the Mandrell Sisters, it ran for two seasons (1981-83) on NBC, with the singer eventually quitting because its time-consuming production cut back on her other activities. Around the same time the network also screened the Nashville Palace programs, as well as booking more country acts for appearances on the Today and Tomorrow shows.

Country also found a welcome in the rapidly developing cable industry, with Showtime setting time aside for the 'Jamboree In The Hills' festival and the 'Tulsa Country Music Festival' as well as 'specials' on the Oak Ridge Boys, Loretta Lynn and Tanya Tucker among others. Home Office (HBO) staked its claims with Kris And Anne (Kristofferson and Murray), Country Music USA (Roy Clark) and George Jones presentations. Arguably the biggest boost for Nashville's music came in early 1983 when the city's own cable station, The Nashville Network, began transmission. Created by WSM Inc and Group W Satellite Communications, the cable was launched into six-million homes with shows that featured all aspects of country in a schedule that also took in comedies, quizzes and other varied items. Also, of course, it provided an outlet for many of Nashville's long-time personalities like deejay and early-

ROSIE'S NASHVILLE
Presents

Above: Jerry Reed *(far left)* made an appearance in the movie *W.W. &*

Left: **Jerry Reed followed up his successful recording career with television and movie productions.**
Below: **Dolly Parton's second musical movie, *The Best Little Whorehouse in Texas,* also starred Burt Reynolds.**
Right: **Burt Reynolds starred in a number of country theme movies, including *Smokey and the Bandit,* and also made his own country recordings.**

morning television-presenter Ralph Emery, who gained the evening's prime-time slot with Nashville Now, and broadcaster/writer Teddy Bart. Among the Nashville Network's other presentations were Bobby Bare And Friends, whose guests were songwriters; Dancin' USA, a current-music program hosted by Jacky Ward; Fire On The Mountain, spotlighting bluegrass and traditional music; Yesteryear In Nashville, hosted by Archie Campbell; and Fandango, a country-music oriented quiz show which provided the most recent television accomplishment for Bill Anderson.

Another area for country singers' developing careers were guest appearances in drama series, with The Fall Guy, Vegas and The Love Boat all regularly drawing upon such talent. Charly McClain made her dramatic debut in Hart To Hart, and The Dukes Of Hazzard (which had Waylon Jennings as its narrator and singer of its hit theme) provided a natural setting for many a country star to sing a song or two. The series' original stars, John Schneider and Tom Wopat, also moved into recording themselves, with the former gaining a substantial hit with *It's Now Or Never* (1981). Another series with a hit tune was Movin' On, the continuing tale of truck drivers played by Claude Akins and Frank Converse. The title song was penned and sung by Merle Haggard. On the other hand Harper Valley PTA was developed from Jeannie C Riley's hot recording and first saw the light of day as a 1978 feature movie starring Barbara Eden.

Above: **Waylon Jennings guitar and voice feature in television's The Dukes of Hazzard.**
Left: **Jerry Reed was introduced into the movies by Burt Reynolds. Today the singer, songwriter and guitarist is an all-round entertainer.**

After Movin' On, the ubiquitous Claude Akins moved on to Nashville 99 (1978), a short-lived crime series filmed in Music City, which co-starred Jerry Reed and utilized many country singers as guests playing themselves. A year later Akins and Reed again joined forces for the Nashville television movie *The Concrete Cowboys* and, that same year, another television movie – *Murder In Music City* (aka *The Country Music Murders*) – was shot in the same location. This light-weight whodunnit starred Sonny Bono, and featured Barbara Mandrell, Charlie Daniels and Ronnie Milsap among its impressive guest list. Also firmly rooted in country was *Stand By Your Man* (1981), television's answer to the cinema's *Coal Miner's Daughter,* which starred Annette O'Toole and told the story of Tammy Wynette.

Naturally, television was quick to seize upon the talents of Kenny Rogers and, besides appearing in a variety of shows, he made his starring debut in *The Gambler* (1980), based upon his million-selling single, and followed up with another 'based upon song' television movie, *Coward Of The County* (1981). (Incidentally, Rogers had made his television movie debut, along with the First Edition, in the 1974 production *The Dream Makers,* starring James Franciscus.) He then moved into motion pictures with *Sixpack* (1982), portraying a race-car driver caught up with a group of kids. The movie gave him another hit in its theme song, *Love Will Turn You Around,* and presented a healthy country sountrack which included the voices of Merle Haggard and Tanya Tucker.

In the realms of the cinema, country soundtracks were a contributing asset to the success of many movies in recent years and, in a number of instances, also provided strong album sales. The

Above: Willie Nelson and Dyan Cannon starred in *Honeysuckle Rose,* which featured Willie Nelson's music.
Right and below: 'Go ahead punk, make my day.' Following his fame as Dirty Harry, Clint Eastwood went on to star in the money-making movie *Every Which Way but Loose.*

Left: **Barbara Mandrell appears with her sisters in her television series, but on stage she performs alone.**
Right: **Dolly Parton provided the hit theme for *9 to 5*.**
Next two pages: **Dolly Parton in concert.**

supreme case was *Urban Cowboy* (1980) for, besides being one of the year's top grossers, it produced an album that sold in excess of four-million copies (and produced a second album, this collecting around 500,000 sales). At the same time, theme tunes could whip up good single sales, like Clint Eastwood's *Every Which Way But Loose* (1978) which provided Eddie Rabbitt the song with which to break into the pop charts, though a country song was not always the means to salvage a bad movie. In the case of *Coast To Coast* (1980), the theme tune could hardly generate enough reaction for a chart appearance for T G Sheppard, a singer who otherwise was chalking up a stack of Number 1 recordings.

It was nothing new to find a country tune as a theme to a movie and, more than twenty years back, when story songs were in vogue, country artists were to be heard at the beginning of a number of westerns, with *High Noon* (1952, Tex Ritter) setting the pace for such as *The Hanging Tree* (1958, Marty Robins), *North To Alaska* (1960, Johnny Horton) and *The Comancheros* (1961, Claude King), while, later, the sound of bluegrass instrumentals added to the excitement of *Bonnie And Clyde* (1967, Lester Flatt & Earl Scruggs) and *Deliverance* (1972, Eric Weissburg and Steve Mandell). As the 1970's country boom developed, some movies were actually created from already proven hit songs, like *Ode To Billy Joe* (1976), *Middle Age Crazy* (1980), *The Night The Lights Went Out In Georgia* (1981), which presented creditable musical performances from its stars Kristy McNichol and Dennis Quaid, and *Take This Job And Shove It* (1982) which contained cameo roles from the song's writer, David Allan Coe, and Lacy J Dalton.

A number of artists were given far greater soundtrack exposure and were heard throughout the movies, with Roger Miller providing his voice and his songs to *Waterhole 3* (1967), and Johnny Cash being heard in a couple of 1970 productions, *I Walk The Line* and *Little Fauss And Big Halsy*. The voice of Tammy Wynette blended in with extracts of classical music in Jack Nicholson's *Five Easy Pieces* (1970), while the recordings of Hank Williams added to the detailed nostalgia conjured up in director Peter Bogdanovich's splendid *The Last Picture Show* (1971). Hank Williams' own life story, somewhat fictionalized, had been filmed several years earlier as *Your Cheatin' Heart* (1964), which starred George Hamilton as the legendary singer and the music voiced over by Hank Williams Jr. A completely fictionalized, and more realistic, view of a country singer and his lifestyle was portrayed by Rip Torn in the hard hitting *Payday* (1972). A decade later, a more compassionate appraisal was presented by Robert Duvall in *Tender Mercies* (1983), which not only displayed the actor convincingly putting over his music but also added up to one of the year's best movies, regardless of subject matter.

There have also been numerous productions which featured real-life country singers, some merely providing an opportunity for the artist to put over his music on the screen while others made determined efforts at acting as an extension to already successful careers. Hollywood, as discussed earlier, had taken an interest in country singers (in addition to their own singing cowboys) during the 1940s, though one of the first of such productions, *Grand Ole Opry* (1940), had locations shot in Nashville and featured Roy Acuff prior to his commencing his Republic deal in the movie capital. By the late 1950s/early 1960s a whole spate of low-budget, country movies was hitting the screens, virtually making use of every chart artist around, and often bearing titles that reflected the swiftness of the shooting schedules. These included such gems as *Hillbillies In A Haunted House, Hootenanny Hoot, Second Fiddle To A Steel Guitar, Still On A Hill, Cottin Pickin' Chicken Pickers, Forty Acre Feud, Country Music Holiday* and *Country Music On Broadway*.

A dozen or so years later, the genre had gained far greater respectability, with Hollywood pumping huge finances into productions that very clearly spelt out a country music message, if not in plots then most certainly in its soundtracks. Curiously, though, the movie industry's first major connections with country music – Kris Kristofferson and *Nashville* – had only the most tenuous links with the music itself. Kristofferson, riding the crest of the songwriting wave, began his succesful movie career with *Cisco Pike* (1972), the tale of a drug-dealing rock musician, and then joined forces with Bob Dylan in the violent *Pat Garrett & Billy The Kid* (1973). Of the many films that this singer/songwriter has now made, only one possessed country-music ingredients – *Convoy* (1978), which was based upon C W McCall's CB trucking hit and featured a soundtrack of country singers – while his appearance in the remake of *A Star Is Born* (1976), with Barbra Streisand, once again cast him as a rock musician. Director Robert Altman's extremely lengthy *Nashville* (1975) was a multistructured affair which linked a Southern political campaign with the music industry, sometimes coming a little too close for comfort to some viewers' thinking and was way off course in its representation of country music.

As far as the Hollywood acting fraternity was concerned, country music found two close allies in Burt Reynolds and Clint Eastwood, both of whom have drawn upon the music in a number of their

Left: The movie *Urban Cowboy* was shot on location at Mickey Gilley's club in Pasadena, Texas. He owns the club jointly with Sherwood Cryer, and has hit the top of the charts with a number of his records.

movies. Reynolds (who actually recorded a country music album, *Ask Me What I Am,* in Nashville in 1973) was the first, with his *W.W. And The Dixie Dancekings* (1975). The movie featured Jerry Reed, Connie Van Dyke and Don Williams in the cast and the plot centered on the fortunes of a country-music band. The Reynolds-Reed partnership continued with *Gator* (1976) and, the following year, the hugely successful *Smokey And The Bandit,* which presented a country-music soundtrack, CB radio, car chases and smash-ups galore, a format the created two equally well-received sequels in 1980 and 1983.

Next to Kristofferson, singer/songwriter/guitarist Jerry Reed (born Atlanta, Georgia, 20 March 1937) was the most successful in making the country music to Hollywood transition. He now has a number of theatrical and television productions to his credit and, like his movie mentor Reynolds, displays an instantly likable personality and off-the-cuff humor. Musical ambitions had loomed first in his mind and, after playing in Atlantic clubs, he scored his initial success when Gene Vincent recorded his *Crazy Legs* (1956) and he secured a contract with Capitol as a rockabilly artist. In the 1960s he settled in Nashville and built up a reputation as a session musician (which inspired his song *Guitar Man,* a 1968 hit for Elvis Presley, as well as giving him another that same year with *U.S. Male,* and writing about him in *Tupelo Mississippi Flash*). He created enough interest for Chet Atkins to sign him to an RCA contract in 1965 and, later, they recorded a couple of guitar albums together. After a handful of chart singles, Reed's own recording career really took off with the crossover hits *Amos Moses* (1970) and *When You're Hot, You're Hot* (1971). This led to a regular spot on Glen Campbell's television show and, in turn, a movie audition in Hollywood. These days Jerry Reed cuts across entertainment areas by making films, heading a hot band of musicians on the road and cutting hit records like *She Got The Goldmine (I Got The Shaft)* (1982) and the novelty *The Bird* (1982).

Clint Eastwood first showed his hand with country music in the phenomenally successful *Every Which Way But Loose* (1978), a slight tale with ingredients comprising brawls, honky tonks, chases and a country-music soundtrack in which the star shared acting honors with an orang-utan. It spawned an equally successful sequel in *Any Which Way You Can* (1980), its soundtrack included a hit theme performed by Glen Campbell and *You're The Reason God Made Oklahoma* (1981), a top chart item that firmly established the reputations of David Frizzell and Shelly West (he Lefty's brother, she the daughter of Dottie). Frizzell and West continued dueting with *Texas State Of Mind* (1981), while also making it as solo acts – Frizzell, who had been recording for several years, with *I'm Gonna Hire A Wino To Decorate Our Home* (1982) and West with *Jose Cuervo* (1983)). *Any Which Way You Can* also established a relationship between Eastwood and long-time record producer/arranger Snuff Garrett, resulting in the revival of Viva Records.

Eastwood continued to push the country sounds in *Bronco Billy* (1980), which resulted in him making a chart appearance dueting with Merle Haggard on *Bar Room Buddies.* In 1982 Eastwood portrayed a 1930s country singer out for an audition on the Grand Ole Opry, failing it and dying of tuberculosis after recording a selection of his songs. The movie was *Honky Tonk Man,* sadly a box-office failure, that also saw appearances by Marty Robbins, Ray Price and fiddle-player Johnny Gimble portraying Bob Wills.

The highly successful careers of Dolly Parton and Willie Nelson took further upward strides with their arrival in motion pictures, both showing that they could handle this medium as well as music. Parton made her debut in *9 To 5* (1980), an amusing comedy that not only gave her a million-selling hit theme but also showed off her bubbling personality to good effect in the company of Jane Fonda and Lily Tomlin. Her next offering was a musical, *The Best Little Whorehouse in Texas* (1982), in which she played opposite Burt Reynolds, and she had another box-office champion, Sylvester Stallone, for her co-star in *Rhinestone* (1984).

Nelson also had a couple of top names around for his debut role in *The Electric Horseman* (1979) – Robert Redford and Jane Fonda – and the movie featured Nelson's music on the soundtrack. However, his next movie, *Honeysuckle Rose* (1980) – a box office disappointment, although it did produce a healthy selling album and a crossover single in *On The Road Again* – saw him taking on an almost biographical role as a country singer and a score of Nelson's own past hit songs. Subsequently he appeared in dramatic roles in *Thief* (1981) and the self-produced *Barbarossa* (1982), while current projects include the long-awaited filming of his *Red Headed Stranger* album concept.

The boom year for country music movies was 1980 and, besides those already mentioned, there was also *Urban Cowboy* and *Coal Miner's Daughter,* both top box-office grossers. *Urban Cowboy* was intended to do for country what *Saturday Night Fever* did for disco and, although it didn't create as much publicity for John Travolta as the earlier film had done, it was trend-setting in the establishment of the urban-cowboy movement as well as being a great promotion for mechanical bulls and Gilley's Club (where the majority of sequences were filmed) in Pasadena, Texas. Based on a short story that originally appeared in Esquire magazine, the movie captured the atmosphere of the Texas honky-tonk nightspot and was enriched with a soundtrack that drew upon the talents of such as the Charlie Daniels Band, the Eagles, Kenny Rogers, Anne Murray, Bonnie Raitt and Linda Ronstadt. It also made a crossover star of Mickey Gilley and launched the career of Johnny Lee.

'*Urban Cowboy* was worth 20 years of paid publicity,' remarked Mickey Gilley (born Ferriday, Louisiana) a couple of years later. A cousin of Jerry Lee Lewis, he moved to Houston, Texas, at the age of seventeen where, after a short stint in the construction business, he decided to try his luck with music and started to work clubs. In time he gained a good reputation, leading on to a recording career that saw him moving through a succession of small labels during a dozen or so years and eventually making his chart debut with *Now I Can Live Again* (1968) on Paula Records. His luck began to change at the beginning of the 1970s when he met up with millionaire Sherwood Cryer who, impressed with the singer-pianist's local reputation, offered him a share of a club he was planning to open. Thus Gilley's came into being. In 1974 Gilley notched up another of his regional hits, *Roomful Of Roses,* only this one was different – it got picked up by Hugh Hefner's Playboy label and, within weeks, it was at the top of the national country charts. Six more Number 1s followed during an equal number of years – including *City Lights* (1975) and *Don't The Girls All Get Prettier At Closing Time* (1976) – as well as several near misses and a change of labels to Epic. In 1980, looking toward the crossover market as a natural extension of his activities, he took on Jim Ed Norman (the man behind Anne Murray's success) as his record producer. At the same time *Urban Cowboy* arrived on the scene. The result was *Stand By Me,* which attracted mass audiences and was a big hit in both country and pop terms.

Texas-born Johnny Lee had also gained a loyal local following before breaking into the bigtime, as well as scoring a number of minor chart successes during the late 1970s, beginning with *Sometimes* (1975). Starting his musical career with a rock 'n' roll band during his high-school days, Lee met Gilley in 1968 and, from there

Above: **Johnny Lee also has his own club, called Johnny Lee's, not far from Mickey Gilley's.**
Left: **Western outlaw Barbarosa, played by Willie Nelson, orders the cantina patrons to surrender their money in the movie *Barbarosa*.**
Next page: **Johnny Lee and Mickey Gilley starred in *Urban Cowboy* together and now do commercials for Schlitz beer.**

on, they built up a friendship and an on-off working relationship. In *Urban Cowboy* they dueted on *Mamas, Don't Let Your Babies Grow Up To Be Cowboys,* but it was Lee's solo *Lookin' For Love* that brought him immediate success – a million-selling country/pop single. It led on to more country chart toppers, including *One In A Million* (1980) and *Bet Your Heart On Me* (1981). These days he has his own club, Johnny Lee's, six miles up the road from Gilley's and, on Valentine's Day 1982, married actress Charlene Tilton (of Dallas fame).

Coal Miner's Daughter was equally as successful a movie, becoming the second biggest grosser of the year, taking some $90 million in domestic revenue during its first twelve months on release. It was one of the few movies to be based on a biography (country superstar Loretta Lynn), and drew a finely detailed, Academy Award-winning performance from its star Sissy Spacek. She spent several months in the company of Lynn prior to the commencement of the movie's filming. Direction was handled by Britain's Michael Apted (who had previously worked on the 1974 David Essex musical *Stardust*), and the characters of Mooney Lynn and Patsy Cline were handled by Tommy Lee Jones and Beverly D'Angelo respectively.

Besides the acting chores, Sissy Spacek also handled all the vocals herself, perfectly re-creating many of Loretta Lynn's most famous songs and resulting not only in a best-selling soundtrack album but also finding the actress in the country charts with the theme song. But that's not really so surprising as, prior to the commencement of her acting career, Spacek had tried her luck at singing in her native Texas. What is a little different though is that, following her convincing performance as a singer in *Coal Miner's Daughter,* Sissy Spacek landed herself a recording deal with Atlantic-America, resulting in the second, high-placed chart single, *Lonely But Only For You* (1983) and the album release *Hangin' Up My Heart* (1983). Now that's something different . . . Hollywood coming to the country-music scene.

Schlitz

Country Today

So country music had reached the 1980s, but who was prepared to define what country was anymore? Its progress through the 1970s had been given a monumental push through the involvement of movies and television, and interest was further generated by the urban cowboy movement which made itself seen through the nation. Suddenly country was very fashionable, and stetsons and boots sneaked into metropolitan attire. Many discos even started to present a brand-new sound. Crossover had reached its outer limits, with the music's most recent successes claiming the mass audience that had been sought through its MOR and rock-styled recordings.

At the same time a reactionary movement was brewing among some deejays and industry sections as well as a number of the more 'country' country singers, who had always expressed such a viewpoint. They thought that crossover had gone too far and the battlecry was out for more hard-core country records to find their way back into radio-station playlists. But, for every Kenny Rogers or Dolly Parton record that wound up a monster hit, there was always a George Jones or Moe Bandy single that was more directly linked to country's roots. And, of course, the Grand Ole Opry still continued to attract capacity audiences, although its past glories and hallowed walls had been somewhat overshadowed by its plush new setting in the lavish Opryland complex.

The new decade continued to bring forth its success stories. Artists who had been achieving regular hits in the country market, like Don Williams, the Oak Ridge Boys and T G Sheppard, suddenly came up with the record that took their music into pop-chart regions, while a whole new generation of country singers – like Janie Fricke, Charly McClain, Earl Thomas Conley and Lacy J. Dalton – proved a liking existed for their music. There was also a place for the different sounds of country, as witnessed by the 1982 and 1983 CMA Male Vocalist award winners Ricky Skaggs and Lee Greenwood, the first bearing a direct link to his bluegrass roots and the other possessing an easy-listening, crossover approach. Hank Williams Jr. showed that he could do it his way, and Alabama established themselves as the country music's biggest phenomenon in recent years.

Don Williams (born Plainview, Texas, 27 May 1939), the 'Gentle Giant of Country Music,' had been scoring hits steadily since 1972, though it wasn't until eight years later that his easeful sounds finally made their mark with a mass audience with *I Believe In You.* Strangely, this wasn't his first connection with the pop charts – that had happened a couple of decades earlier when, as a member of the Pozo-Seco Singers (with Susan Taylor and Lofton Cline), the group found glory with their folk-pop sounds with songs such as *I Can Make It With You* (1966). After they split up Williams returned to his native Texas but, upon the encouragement of his close friends Jack Clement and Allen Reynolds (who had worked together since Clement had engineered at Sun, and weaved a musical course that took them from Memphis to Texas to Nashville), Williams began a solo career on the recently launched JMI label with *The Shelter Of Your Eyes* (1972). During the next few years he established a reputation with some of country's most memorable, and attractive, songs – including *Amanda* (1972), *You're My Best Friend* (1975), *'Til The Rivers All Run Dry* (1976) and *Tulsa Time* (1978) – while moving labels to ABC/Dot and MCA. His stage performances are as memorable as his records; his quiet, precise vocals and instrumentation communicates directly to his audiences. It was such performances that earned him his loyal following and gained high, critical acclaim in Britain (where he was the recipient of many Gold Discs before his success in the States). It's not uncommon to find audiences taking over on the vocals from the singer.

The Oak Ridge Boys claim equally loyal support, though their stage performances are virtually at the other end of the spectrum, a fast-paced showcase with dynamic, almost choreographed presentations from each of the group's four members. Following on from their pop chart breakthrough with the two-million selling *Elvira* (1981), and the follow-up *Bobbie Sue* (1982), the quartet now commands attention across the board, from teenagers to dyed-in-the-wool country fans. But it wasn't always that way. Originally a gospel music act, with roots stretching back some 40 years to Oak Ridge, Tennessee, the current lineup comprises Duane Allen (lead), Joe Bonsall (tenor), Richard Sterban (bass) and William Lee Golden (baritone, the longest serving member, he joined in 1964). They made the move over to country in 1975 and, within a couple of years, *Y'all Come Back Saloon* commenced a nonstop run of country successes. Others have included *I'll Be True To You* (1978), *Leaving Louisiana In The Broad Day Light* (1979), *Trying To Love Two Women* (1980), *American Made* (1983) and *Love Song* (1983). Their success encompasses several awards that take in a 1982 Grammy and three CMA accolades. They also head a versatile six-piece band as well as their own corporate business, based in Hendersonville (some 20 miles north of Nashville), that takes in music publishing, recording and merchandizing.

T G. Sheppard (born Humbolt, Texas, 20 July 1944) made the ultimate crossover with *I Love 'Em Every One* in 1981, just one of

Right: **One of country music's most-booked session singers, Janie Fricke is now one of country music's top female singers in her own right.**

Right: **Don Williams, the 'Gentle Giant of Country Music,' takes in his audience's warm response.**

several singles that leaned heavily toward a MOR/pop audience and reaped the rewards of success that had commenced with a Number 1 record on a brand-new label. That was back in 1974 with *The Devil In The Bottle,* a single released on Motown's short-lived country outlet Melodyland (later to be rechristened Hitsville). Sheppard's connections with music, though, had begun many years earlier, in the early 1960s when – recording under the name of Brian Stacy on Atlantic – he scored a minor pop hit with *High School Days.* Later, reverting back to his real name of Bill Browder, he moved over to the business side of the music industry, first working as promotions man for RCA in Memphis (where he built up a friendship with Presley, among others) and then developing his own organization. That's when *The Devil* came into the picture, a song that he was convinced would be a hit but, as he couldn't find an artist to share his belief, he recorded it himself – and created the name T G Sheppard at the same time. With his faith in the song confirmed, he continued the hit pattern with *Tryin' To Beat The Morning Home* (1975) and *Motel And Memories* (1975) and, after moving on to Warner Bros., quickly established himself as one of the foremost members of country's contemporary movement with such as *Mister D.J.* (1977), *Last Cheater's Waltz* (1979), *I'll Be Coming Home To You* (1979), *Do You Wanna Go To Heaven* (1980), *Finally* (1982) and *Slow Burn* (1983). These days he's one of the music's most consistent Number 1 record makers.

Another artist who weaved a crossover path for three decades and has now built an entirely new career in the country market is B J Thomas. He first charted with a Hank Williams' song, *I'm So Lonesome I Could Cry* (1966), but found international fame and fortune with *Raindrops Keep Fallin' On My Head* (1969), from the top-grossing movie *Butch Cassidy And The Sundance Kid.* Then he started making a move back into country with *(Hey Won't You Play) Another Somebody Done Somebody Wrong Song* (1975) before entering a period of recording mainly gospel music and writing two best-selling autobiographies with his wife Gloria – *Home Where I Belong* and *In Tune.* These days he's a proud member of the Grand Ole Opry and chart topper with such as *Whatever Happened To Old Fashioned Love* (1983) and *New Looks From An Old Lover* (1983).

For the fans who liked pure country music, there were a couple of newcomers who quickly joined the ranks of Bandy, Bruce and Watson. John Anderson, who first started getting his name around in 1979 (after a couple of years on Warner Bros) with *Low Dog Blues* and *Your Lying Blues Eyes,* brought the strains of rich vocals and pure country styling into the midst of the crossover movement's most active period – and found soon he was winning praise from deejays and fans alike. This Florida-born singer/songwriter quickly moved into the higher chart regions with *1959* (1980) and *I'm Just An Old Chunk Of Coal* (1981) and, in 1983, achieved one of the music's biggest singles of the year with the million-selling *Swingin'.* Meanwhile Texas rancher George Strait kept up his home state's fine honky-tonk traditions as he broke into the national limelight in 1981 with *Unwound* and *Down And Out,* while moving right to the top the following year with *Fool Hearted Memory* and *Marina Del Ray.* Raised to the sounds of country music, he first sang in a country band during his time with the Army in Hawaii and started working with a band of musicians (the nucleus for his current-day Ace In The Hole Band) in his off-duty hours from the ranch.

Another singer with a highly distinctive vocal styling is Kentucky-born John Conlee, a one-time mortician turned rock deejay who made his name stick in 1978 with *Rose Colored Glasses* and *Lady*

***Left and above:* Don Williams has contributed a string of attractive songs during the last ten years. He has a quiet and appealing stage presence.**

Lay Down. To date he's scored some twenty hits, a couple of the more recent being *Common Man* (1983) and *In My Eyes* (1983). Vern Gosden had been around for a far longer period, having made his chart debut with his brother Rex (as the Gosden Brothers) with *Hangin' On* (1967), before achieving solo success almost ten years later with a string of releases on Elektra. But in 1983 he became the subject of much public and industrial acclaim when, on Compleat Records, he went straight to the top with *If You're Gonna Do Me Wrong (Do It Right),* a song that gained itself – and him – CMA nominations and heralded the commencement of a bright, new country career. But possibly the most unique success story of them all is that of Boxcar Willie, the Texas-based singer who takes on a hobo guise and sings in the best Jimmie Rodgers' and Hank Williams' traditions, as well as re-creating the sound of train whistles to perfection. He's another entertainer whose career first blossomed in Britain, then started hitting the American market

Above: **John Conlee got started in 1978 with** ***Rose Colored Glasses.***
Above left: **Rodney Crowell, singer in his own right and husband of Rosanne Cash.**
Right: **B J Thomas was a crossover artist who now concentrates on country music and is a member of the Grand Ole Opry.**

through a top-selling television album. At the beginning of 1983 he began his singles career in earnest with *The Man I Used To Be.*

Producer Billy Sherrill, one of the key figures of the crossover movement, was still keeping very busy although, by the early 1980s, he had left his executive post at Columbia and was working an independent production deal for the label. But he still maintained his role as a major discoverer of talent, and one of his great finds, Janie Fricke, was right at the top of the ladder, having been voted Female Vocalist of the Year by CMA members for both 1982 and 1983. Born near South Whitney, Indiana, Fricke made her first contact with the music business by recording jingles in Memphis between studies at the Indiana University, and then headed out west to try her luck in Los Angeles. She soon returned to Memphis, where the pickings were more lucrative and remained there until 1975 when she headed to Nashville and earned herself a place in one of the city's busiest vocal groups, The Lea Jane Singers. It was through her solo work on Johnny Duncan's *Jo And The Cowboy* (1975) that she came to the attention of Sherrill, and the producer made more use of her voice on the subsequent Duncan recordings, *Stranger,* penned by Kris Kristofferson, and *Thinkin' Of A Rendezvous,* both high charters in 1976. The Fricke tones were to be heard on other Number 1s that same year, including Tanya Tucker's *Here's Some Love,* Ronnie Milsap's *Let My Love Be Your Pillow* and Crystal Gayle's *I'll Get Over You.* By then Billy Sherrill had decided to give the lady a chance in her own right; the result was her chart debut with *What're You Doing Tonight* (1977). Since then the hits have continued to flow her way and include *Down To My Last Broken Heart* (1980), *I'll Need Someone To Hold Me When I Cry* (1981), *Do Me With Love* (1982) and *He's A Heartache* (1983). Besides making her own records, and keeping up a hectic road schedule, she still finds time to slot in the occasional session as backup singer and, to date, has notched up over 5000 of them as well as countless jingles for organizations such as United Airlines, Red Lobster Restaurants and the Third National Bank.

Another of Billy Sherrill's major discoveries is Pennsylvania-born Lacy J Dalton, although her success is not of the overnight variety. The possessor of a gravelly, bluesy voice, she first tried her luck as a folk protest singer in the Midwest during her teens and, at 21, was leading Office, a psychedelic rock 'n' roll band in North California. For a while she worked under the name of Jill Corston and it was a copy of a privately produced album she recorded that caught Sherrill's attention. Reputedly, the resultant record deal was one of the fastest ever. The releases that followed not only displayed the singer's skill in handling a wide range of material but are also a tribute to the producer, who wasn't afraid to experiment in order to seek out the best for her voice. She made her debut in a straight country vein with *Crazy Blue Eyes* (1979) and *Tennesssee Waltz* (1980); started making effective use of her distinctive styling on *Hard Times* (1980); moved into easy listening with *Takin' It Easy* (1981); and took a more deliberate aim at country-pop crossover with a revival of Roy Orbison's *Dream Baby* (1983). Among her other top successes was a fine tribute to Nashville's music community, *16th Avenue* (1982).

Perhaps one of the most amazing of country's recent success stories is that of Indiana-born Sylvia, who possessed no musical experience prior to her knocking on Nashville doors and ending up as a secretary to top producer/publisher Tom Collins. Then she started studying recording techniques, sat in on a few sessions as a background singer and failed an audition with Dave & Sugar but impressed RCA and Charley Pride enough for Collins to secure her a contract with the label. She made her chart debut with *You Don't Miss A Thing* (1979), reached the Top 10 with *Tumbleweed* (1980) and arrived at the top with *Drifter* (1981). It was only a short step away from the crossover market, reached in 1982 with the attractive pop-styled *Nobody.*

Among the other women who have been building their popularity steadily is Tennessee's Charly McClain. She began entertaining at the age of nine (then heading a band named Charlotte and The Volunteers) and gained a deal with Epic, eleven years later, through the efforts of Memphis producer Larry Rogers. Her fast-mounting array of hits include *Men* (1980) and the Number 1s *Who's Cheatin' Who* (1981), *Sleepin' With The Radio On* (1982) and the Mickey Gilley duet *Paradise* (1983). Reba McEntire, from Chockie, Oklahoma, was Mercury's top country female until moving to MCA in 1984, though ranching and rodeoing are almost as important to her as music. Discovered by Red Steagall, she built her reputation upon her pure vocal styling and memorable hits like *(You Lift Me) Up To Heaven* (1980), *Today All Over Again* (1981), *I'm Not That Lonely Yet* (1982) and achieved her first chart topper with *Can't Even Get The Blues* (1982). Blind since birth, singer/pianist Terri Gibbs blended her music with a soulful voice and a touch of blues, and wound up with a Top 10 MCA debut with *Somebody's Knockin'* (1980). Subsequent hits include *Rich Man* (1981) and *Mis'ry River* (1982). Oklahoma's Gail Davies' influences combine country, pop and jazz, though her initial chart successes, *Poison Love* (1978), *Blue Heartache* (1979) and *I'll Be There (If You Ever Want Me)* (1980), were more directly linked to traditional country roots. By 1983, though, her recordings (which she also produces for Warner Bros.) were taking on a much stronger country-pop direction.

Two females very successful in the crossover stakes were Juice Newton and Rosanne Cash. The former, who hails from Virginia but had been performing music on the West Coast since the early 1970s with her Silver Spur Band, made a minor chart impression with *Love Is A Word* (1976) but, with a move to Capitol, made the international bigtime with *Angel Of The Morning* (1981) and *The Sweetest Thing* (1981). Rosanne Cash carried on her famous father's traditions of both country and pop success and, after gaining industry experience (by working in CBS Records, London) and studying drama at Nashville's Vanderbilt University and Los Angeles' Lee Strasburg Theater Institute, she made her record debut (strangely) on Germany's Ariola label. But it was through signing a deal with Columbia that she gained success, first as a duet partner to Bobby Bare on *No Memories Hangin' Around* (1976) and then on to the crossover market with the top-selling *Seven Year Ache* (1981). She then followed up with more Number 1s in *My Baby Thinks He's A Train* (1981) and *Blue Moon With A Heartache* (1982). Further success runs in the family as she's married to Rodney Crowell, a former member of Emmylou Harris' Hot Band, who now rates as one of Nashville's most successful contemporary songwriters and record producers as well as being a recording artist for Warner Bros.

The ever-changing face of country music is well realized in the Country Music Association's annual awards which, based on members' votes and always reflecting the industry's success stories, had in the past been presented to artists with several years of glory behind them. But, as the 1980s progressed, such reckoning changed dramatically as Alabama, Ricky Skaggs and Lee Greenwood all scooped top accolades with only a handful of hits to their credit. Such was the testament to these artists' success.

Ricky Skaggs (born Cordell, Kentucky, 18 July 1954) delighted the traditionalists, as well as winning over many others, by clearly proving that there was still a place in the charts for the purer sounds of country. He was a child prodigy, raised in family of bluegrass musicians, who had appeared on Lester Flatt & Earl Scrugg's Nashville television show by the age of seven and, at fifteen, had earned himself a place in Ralph Stanley's band. Within the next ten

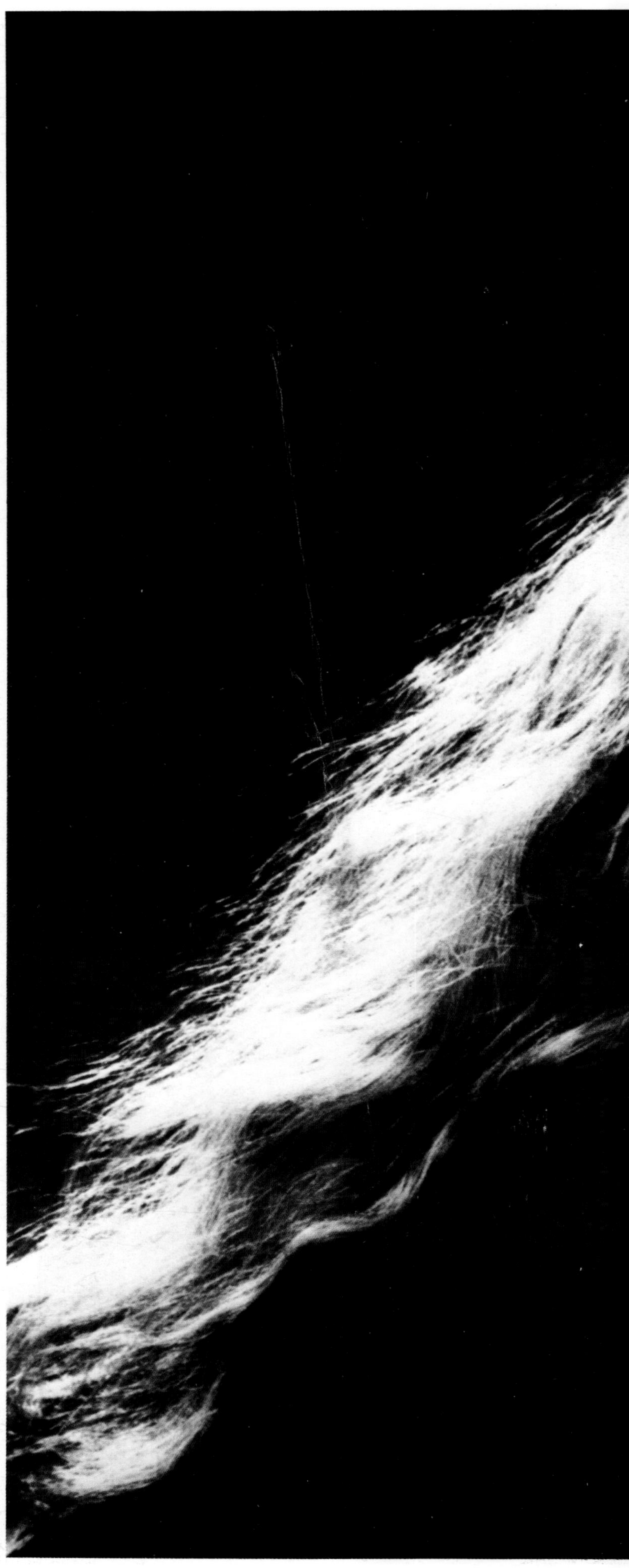

Right: ***Angel of the Morning*** **brought Juice Newton international fame.**

years he built up his bluegrass reputation by working with the Country Gentlemen, J. D. Crowe and the New South as well as leading his own outfit, Boone Creek. Then, at the age of 25, with six albums to his credit, he joined Emmylou Harris' Hot Band and quickly gained attention with country, rock and international audiences as well as being the innovative force behind Emmylou's outstanding *Roses In The Snow* (1980) album.

In 1981, having left Harris and leading his own highly talented group of musicians, he was signed to Columbia and made his chart debut with the Top 20 single *Don't Get Above Your Raisin'*, an old Flatt and Scruggs' number. A little more than twelve months later he had two Number 1s, *Crying My Heart Out Over You* and *I Don't Care*, and two CMA Awards (Male Vocalist and Horizon) to his credit. His success, which has continued with more top singles such as *Heartbroke* (1982) and *Don't Cheat In Our Hometown* (1983), makes a stand for the music's solid traditions. His pure country styling and the sharp instrumentation of his accompanying musicians has not only brought a breath of fresh air to the country charts but has also won the attention of pop and rock audiences. Skaggs has also played a major role in bringing to attention another bluegrass act, The Whites, which features Buck White, his daughters Sharon (to whom Skaggs is married) and Cheryl, and dobro picker Jerry Douglas. Besides regularly working with the CMA award winner, the group also made chart impressions, with

Left: Ricky Skaggs started out in bluegrass and has a pure country style.
Right: Earl Thomas Conley discovered country music in the army.

You Put The Blue In Me (1982) and *Give Me Back That Old Familiar Feeling* (1983) among their releases.

At the other end of country's spectrum Los Angeles-born, Sacramento-raised Lee Greenwood secured a firm foundation for his kind of music. He played Dixieland, rock, soul and country at the Las Vegas nightclubs, displaying his multi-instrumental skills (piano, guitar, saxophone and bass). Like Skaggs, he spent many years paying his dues – in his case, twenty years – before he became an 'overnight sensation' by taking his debut single *It Turns Me Inside Out* (1981) into the Top 20. The son of half-Cherokee parents, he arrived in the Nevada nightclub capital in the early 1960s, and formed his own band, Apollo, later to become The Lee Greenwood Affair. But things weren't easy and, after an ill-fated association with Paramount Records in LA, he returned to Vegas where he worked in various occupations – including music arranger, writer, backup singer, barroom pianist and casino card dealer – though never losing the determination of someday making it in the music business.

It was Mel Tillis' bass player/bandleader, Larry McFaden, who became aware of Greenwood's talents and, after recording a demo session, set about fixing a label deal. That's where MCA came into the picture. Following his chart breakthrough, the singer increased his status with *Ring On Her Finger (Time On Her Hands)* (1982), *Ain't No Trick* (1982) and *I.O.U.* (1983) (nominated as CMA Song of the Year) and, after collecting CMA's Male Vocalist Award, went straight to the top with *Somebody's Gonna Love You* (1983). A few months later he collected his first Grammy Award. The singles tell one side of the story, his stage performances tell another. Standing ovations now greet his skills as an entertainer and it's pretty obvious that he's set for even bigger rewards in the years to come.

Part-time philosopher and poet Earl Thomas Conley, one of the music's most creative singer/songwriters, has also made it as a top-charting artist although he's yet to claim any major awards. Born in Portsmouth, Ohio, he left an impoverished background at the age of 17 and began life on the road, spending time traveling across the States as an artist, sculptor and poet. Then, during his army service in Germany, he came across country music, which led him to club work in Alabama and, finally, to taking his crack at Nashville. He gained initial success as a writer, with singers Billy Larkin, Mel Street and Conway Twitty cutting his original songs, and made his own chart debut in 1975 with *I Have Loved You Girl* on GRT Records. By the beginning of the 1980s he was on another minor label, Sunbird, enjoying Top 10 success with *Silent Treatment* (1980) and, as *Fire And Smoke* (1981) went to Number 1, a new deal was struck with RCA. From then on he's remained a top-chart artist with *Tell Me Why* (1982), *Heavenly Bodies* (1982) and *Your Love's On The Line* (1983) revealing that his country imaginatively combines elements of rock.

RCA had other contemporary singers in Razzy Bailey and Leon Everette, the first struggling for success over a two-decade period before Dickey Lee took one of his earlier-penned songs, *9,999,999 Tears,* and made it a hit in 1976 which, in turn, caused the label to take interest in the writer. Bailey scored his own chart breakthrough with *What Time Do You Have To Be Back To Heaven* in 1978 and, a couple of years later, was at Number 1 with *Loving Up A Storm* and *I Keep Coming Back.* South Carolina-born Leon Everette first took note of country while in the Navy, though one of his first successes was a Presley tribute, *The King Of Rock 'n' Roll* (1977). Within three years he was firmly entrenched in the RCA roster with songs like *Giving Up Easy* (1980), *Hurricane* (1981) and *Midnight Rodeo* (1981) in the Top 10. Also scoring success on the label is Steve Wariner, one-time musician for Dottie West and Bob Luman, and one of the last artists to be produced by Chet Atkins. He made his chart debut with *I'm Already Taken* (1978) and first achieved the top slot with *All Roads Lead To You* (1981).

Native Tennessean Ronnie McDowall, who had developed the art of impersonation during his time in the Navy, put such skills to good use on the most successful of the Presley tributes, *The King Is Gone* (1977), a million-selling crossover that launched him to the public but took a little time to shake off its novelty value. These days, on Epic, he's firmly secured his own status with top hits like *Step Back* (1982) and *You're Gonna Ruin My Bad Reputation* (1983). A couple of singers with powerful voices were, by the early 1980s, making themselves mainstream figures – Con Hunley and Gary Morris. Hunley first gained attention with *Breaking Up Is Hard To Do* (1977) and, five years later, was receiving the country and pop marketing approach with *Oh Girl* (1982). Gary Morris arrived in country from rock and makes use of immaculately arranged close harmonies as part of his stage routines. His successes include *Headed For A Heartache* (1981), *Don't Look Back* (1982) and *Why Lady Why* (1983).

Two trend-setting acts that are the lifeblood of the contemporary movement are Hank Williams Jr. and Alabama, the first carrying on the family tradition and the second launching a tradition of its own.

The greatest problem that faced Hank Williams Jr. (born Shreveport, Louisiana, 26 May 1949) was having a legend for a father – and he said as much in his song *Standing In The Shadows (Of A Very Famous Man)* (1965), one of his earliest chart successes. He had had the music around him since his birth and was pushed into a music career by his mother Audrey, who was determined that he'd be a star. He had made his first Grand Ole Opry appearance

All pictures: Hank Williams, Jr., son of the legend, seen at the left with his pet cat and at the right in performance, forsook the urban lights of Nashville for less congested Alabama. He has come to speak for the nonurban country boy who, 'from North California and South Alabama and little towns all around this land,' have their shotguns, rifles and four-wheel drives, and as Hank, Jr. sings, 'a country boy will survive.'

Above: **Alabama has received virtually all of the major music awards and achieved record sales of albums.**
Right: **Hank Williams, Jr. made a comeback and established his own sound after a near-fatal accident in the mid-1970s.**

by the age of eight and, by sixteen, was a chart name and a major touring attraction – though everyone saw him as Hank's son and they all wanted him to sing Hank's songs. Even his father's record label, MGM, initially viewed him that way. However, by the late 1960s, he was scoring hits that gave him his own identity – *It's All Over But The Crying* (1968), *Cajun Baby* (1969) and his first Number 1 *All For The Love Of Sunshine* (1970) – while his fast-paced stage performances were liberally laced with good old-fashioned rock 'n' roll. But the lifestyle and the cloning had taken its effect, leading a psychiatrist to remark that 'he had fully taken over the image of Hank Williams, the only difference being that Hank Jr. would probably die by the time he reached his 26th year.' He quit Nashville and headed south to Cullman, Alabama, where he linked up with a life-time fishing and hell-raisin' buddy named James R Smith (now his manager) and set about making the music that mattered to him.

He launched into his new career with the *Hank Williams Jr. And Friends* (1975) album, a highly successful blending of country and southern rock which made use of the talents of Charlie Daniels and Toy Caldwell and contained the hit *Stoned At The Jukebox.* But before he could build up in his new directions, disaster struck in an accident that saw the singer falling 500 feet down a Montana mountain. (The accident, the near-fatal injuries and his road to recovery are vividly recounted in his autobiography *Living Proof,* co-penned with Michael Bane.) His survival strengthened his resolve to succeed in his own right and, after several minor chart successes, he broke into the higher regions with *Family Tradition* (1979), a song that laid his thinking clearly on the line. From then on success was his, with hits like *Whiskey Bent And Hell Bound* (1979), *Women I've Never Had* (1980), *Old Habits* (1980), *All My Rowdy Friends* (1981) and *A Country Boy Can Survive* (1982), leading on to the amazing feat of having eight albums in Billboard's Country Charts at the same time, and his sell-out concert appearances taking on the intensity and frenzy of a rock performance. Hank Jr. bucked the system and did it his way – even on occasion recording with other rebels, like supporter and close-friend Waylon Jennings on *The Conversation* (1979), and with Waylon and that original Texas outlaw, Ernest Tubb, on *Leave Them Boys Alone* (1983). Yet, shamefully, in spite of his astonishing success Hank Williams Jr. still hadn't won any major award by the beginning of 1983. Perhaps that's because he *has* followed the family tradition of being a very unique individual and remaining outside of the establishment.

Alabama, on the other hand, have just about won every major award that's going, having been named CMA Entertainers Of The Year for two consecutive years (1982 and 1983) as well as collecting six other CMA awards in a three-year period. Their record success is even more phenomenal and, in the four years since their signing with RCA in 1980, they've achieved a dozen Number 1 records (out of the dozen singles released), insured that all five of their albums have remained in the charts – and mounted sales that neared the twelve-million mark. Alabama is, regardless of all music classification, the supergroup of the era.

But the times haven't always been that magnificent and success didn't happen overnight. The group first saw the light of day as Wild Country, and the wheels were set in motion in Fort Payne, Alabama, as cousins Jeff Cook, who worked for Western Electric, Randy Owen, still at school, and Teddy Gentry, who laid carpets, decided to jam together in late 1969. They eventually worked up

good-enough routines to earn weekend gigs at the local Canyonland Park and there, while watching artists like Bobby Bare, Jerry Wallace and Cal Smith, their thoughts first turned to making a professional career out of music. In March 1973 they started to make their ambitions a reality; they quit their jobs, headed out to Myrtle Beach, South Carolina, and began working the local clubs. Soon they were perfecting their stage routines, bringing original material into their repertoire and, as local success grew, began recording and pressing their own discs for selling at the shows and sending out to the record stations.

In 1977, after getting turned down by virtually every record company in Nashville, they were signed by GRT and made a minor chart entry with *I Wanna Be With You* – but they soon were forgotten in the excitement of the label's major successes. It took another couple of years to catch another company's attention, this time the Dallas-based MDJ Records, and its owner Larry McBride scheduled them to a Nashville recording session with producer Harold Shedd. Then Alabama's drummer abruptly quit. After a month of frantic searching, Mark Herndon entered the picture – and he was to prove the catalyst that put the band in top gear.

Their first single under the MDJ deal, *I Wanna Come Over* (1979), peaked at Number 33 in the Billboard charts; their second, *My Home's In Alabama* (1980), at Number 17; and, in April 1980, as all the record companies that had originally turned them down began to take serious notice, Alabama signed on the dotted line with RCA. By the year's end they had begun their run of Number 1s with *Tennessee River* and *My Home's In Alabama.* Around this time Randy Owen, lead vocalist and rhythm guitarist, reflected 'We really never though we'd be here today. One year ago we were about as low as you can get but, instead of giving up, we decided the only way was up and start over again.' Cousin Teddy Gentry added, 'We spent years to get to this point, but only months for it all to fall into place.'

Three years later the success story appears unflagging. Their concerts are always sellouts and the audience reaction always fever-pitched, the screams of adoration frequently covering over the sounds of the band itself. Alabama's is the biggest country success story of the 1980s to date, and recalled in the few short words of hit titles – *Why Lady Why* (1980), *Old Flame* (1981), *Feels So Right* (1981), *Love In The First Degree* (1981), *Mountain Music* (1982), *Take Me Down* (1982), *Close Enough To Perfect* (1982), *Dixieland Delight* (1983), *The Closer You Get* (1983), *Lady Down On Love* (1983) and *Roll On Eighteen Wheeler* (1983). The songs tell it all.

There's just one other aspect of the Alabama success story that's relevant to the development of country music in general. Alabama brought about another change and set a new trend. They created a new sound, the group sound; the sound of a tight, small unit of singers and musicians rather than the time-old formula of the singer accompanied by musicians. By their success, Alabama has opened up the doorway to others like Bandana, McGuffey Lane, Atlanta and Exile.

And, perhaps, change is the most lasting characteristic of the music itself. After all, throughout its entire commercial history, country has been beset by one change after another, yet survived them all and, often, built upon the changes, to its greater glory. Maybe it's because of its adaptability that country music has remained a continuing success story.

'Lordy I have loved some ladies and I have loved Jim Beam,' sings Hank Williams, Jr., and they both tried to kill him back in 1973. When the doctor asked him how he had gotten in his condition, he said, 'Hey, sawbones, I'm just carryin' on an old family tradition,' a reference to his father's ultimately fatal weakness.

Index

Numbers in italics refer to illustrations.

Acknowledgments

The author is indebted to two invaluable reference works – Bill C Malone's *Country Music USA* and Robert Shelton & Burt Goldblatt's *The Country Music Story* – as well as inspired assistance from Country Music Magazine's *Illustrated History of Country Music* and Richard Wootton's *Country Almanac*. And, of course, this book would never have been completed without the outstanding skills of David Redfern whose photographs have provided images to the words.

Finally my sincere thanks to the numerous artists, record producers and other industry executives whose time and efforts have been the source for countless features over the years. My thanks to them all – and for the good friendships that have developed out of initial business contacts.

Picture Credits
All photographs used in this book have been supplied by the Country Music Foundation Library and Media Center, Nashville, Tennessee, except for the following:

American Graphic Systems Archives: 2-3, 38-39, 52 (top), 108, 109
Bison Picture Library: 145, 147
Jerry Ohlingers: 183, 184-85, 186 (bottom), 187, 190 (both), 190-91, 193, 198-99
RCA: 216
David Redfern: 1, 18 (both), 18-19, 20-21 (top), 22, 35, 42 (all three), 42-43, 50-51, 55, 58, 58-59, 60-61, 61, 62 (both), 63 (both), 64 (top), 65, 66 (all three), 67 (top left), 68-69, 70 (both), 71, 77 (bottom), 78 (all four), 78-79, 82, 82-83, 86 (both), 87, 88-89, 90-91, 91 (both), 93 (top), 94-95, 95, 98 (both), 98-99, 101, 102-03, 103 (both), 106, 107 (all three), 110-11, 114, 118, 120-21, 121, 122 (all four), 123 (top and bottom right), 124-25, 126 (both), 128-29, 130-31, 133, 136, 138, 139 (both), 142-43, 143, 146, 149 (right), 150, 151 (both), 154-55, 155 (left), 159, 160, 162-63, 164-65, 166-67, 169 (right), 170-71, 171 (both), 174 (all four), 175, 178-79, 181, 194, 195, 203, 204-05, 206-07, 207, 218-19, 224
Nashville Area Chamber of Commerce: 14-15, 20-21 (bottom), 23, 74-75, 96, 123 (bottom left), 178, 186 (top), 223
James R. Smith Management: 214, 215, 217
Evelyn B. Stigall: 11 (both)
Bill Yenne: 36, 44 (bottom), 45 (bottom), 46, 50 (bottom), 59 (top left), 81, 118-19, 134, 134-35, 135, 161 (left), 177, 214-15, 219

Next page: Long-time favorite Marty Robbins was a singer, songwriter, musician, actor and businessman before he died in 1982.